REX

REX

AN AUTOBIOGRAPHY BY

WILLIAM MORROW & COMPANY, INC.
New York   1975

Printed in the United States of America.

1 2 3 4 5 79 78 77 76 75

Design by Lucy Fehr

Library of Congress Cataloging in Publication Data

Harrison, Rex.
  Rex; an autobiography.

  1. Harrison, Rex. I. Title.
PN2598.H336A37   791′.092′4 [B]   74-16451
ISBN 0-688-02881-0

Frontispiece: Elizabeth and Rex with Homer at Beauchamp, 1974 (Photo: David Rutherston)

To Elizabeth

Contents

List of Illustrations

The photographs by Angus McBean are reproduced by permission of the Harvard Theatre Collection. Three photographs have been kindly lent by Arthur Barbosa. The photograph on the front of the jacket is by courtesy of Twentieth Century–Fox and that on the back by Pictorial Press Ltd.

Prologue

I have been in the theatre for fifty years and, although I make no pretense of having enjoyed every one of them, it has been and is being a good life for me. In the course of those years a great deal, good and bad, has been written about me and about my work by professional writers and I've often had the uneasy feeling that perhaps other people know more about me than I do. One of my hopes therefore in deciding to write an autobiography was to find out more about the subject, and that is why I preferred to do it myself rather than give the job to an expert. The subject cannot be said to be totally thrilled with his discoveries, but at least he cannot blame anybody else for distorting the truth.

Portofino, Italy, 1974   R.H.

CHAPTER ONE

Act One, Scene One

I felt my first romantic urge when I was about six. We were living then in the village of Huyton, near Liverpool; the nursery in our house was on the top floor, and from the window I could see the far larger house of a family called Brunner, in grounds which amounted to a small estate. Sheila Brunner was a year or two older than I, with lovely long hair which, to my mind, compensated for an undeniably skinny figure—I decided philosophically that one couldn't have everything. We played together quite often, and used to bathe in one of the ponds in the grounds of Sheila's house, both of us in our birthday suits. The water was black with mud and tadpoles, but to me it was crystal clear as I watched Sheila swimming about, her long hair trailing in the water. I was crazy about her.

I can still recall the ecstasy of walking home with Sheila after our first illicit swim. Before long I decided to play truant from the kindergarten school at which my mother deposited me each day. I would hide in the coalhole until all the children had gone into school and then make my way back to Sheila's house, keeping well out of my mother's sight.

That was an idyllic time, running about the cornfields and

13

jumping stark naked into tadpole-infested ponds. What made it all the more marvelous to me was that it was strictly forbidden. I was the runaway with his girl. The summer days flew like lightning until, inevitably, we were found out.

My parents bore down on us, my mother hysterical, my father distant and livid. As a punishment I was to be kept away from my kindergarten for a week. This seemed no sort of punishment to me, until the awful truth was made clear: I was to be confined to barracks, shut up in the house, and not allowed to see Sheila. I really loved that girl. Trying to occupy myself, I climbed a large and dangerous tree in the garden and deliberately made myself filthy tinkering with my tricycle chain. Finally, out of sheer frustration, I hit myself on the head with a two-pronged hammer. To my horror the prongs remained embedded in my forehead, and I have two small scars to this day.

At Penmaenmawr in North Wales, where I was taken for the summer holiday, my longing for Sheila was offset by desperate efforts to get warm after bathing in the bitter Irish Sea. I shall never forget the size of my goosepimples, or the sugary buns I was fed to warm me up. I think my dramatic leanings first made themselves apparent then, as I began to realize what a splendid nuisance I could be. I delighted in hiding myself in the bracken on our long walks, lying in wait for my two sisters and my parents and then jumping out at them, screaming my head off and making fiendish grimaces.

One day I was walking ahead of my parents, alongside a particularly pretty wall, all mossy stone and lichen, when I became aware of a heated conversation from which I was definitely excluded. They would pause as the argument grew livelier, so I too hung back, trying hard to overhear. I caught words like "war" and "Germany," which meant little to me, but I was quick enough to perceive that my father was furious at having his holiday disturbed, while my mother obviously thought he ought to be taking things more seriously. It was August, 1914.

My attention soon shifted to more important matters, such as candy stores and beach balls, but the argument would suddenly break out again, my mother urging my father to take some sort of action and my father refusing to upset himself. This was, as I learned in later life, a fairly strong indication of his character.

I think my father's lack of ambition had something to do with my own urge to succeed. He was a tall, straight-backed man whom I always remember with a cornflower, the Harrow school flower, in the buttonhole of his Norfolk jacket. He had played hockey for England and run the hundred yards in 10.5 seconds, and had studied engineering in Germany, but throughout his life he did very little work—I think because there was nothing he really wanted to do. He was a great companion on holidays, and endlessly patient when trying to teach me to play games: he spent hours bowling to me in the hope of making me a good cricketer. But although he was marvelous with us as children, after my sisters and I were over a certain age he seemed to lose interest in us.

My father was the third son of a large family, seven boys and a girl, and had grown up in a country house with its own stables and tennis courts and a cricket ground. My mother, whose maiden name was Carey, also came from a large family of boys and had played a good deal of tennis with her brothers and my father when he was courting her.

Even at a tender age I was a great admirer of my mother's looks, her ample bust and fine big hips. The male/female had not then come into vogue and I remember observing her figure with pleasure when she came to tuck me in. I also remember a pleasant smell of scent, and—I must have disturbed her from a dinner party—a most agreeable whiff of an excellent Bordeaux. She was patient and protective, and I loved her. I heard quite a few rows between my mother and father—what child doesn't?—and mostly, it seemed, about me.

When I was seven we moved to Sheffield, and I had to say good-bye to Sheila. I can remember feeling shy and almost de-

My mother

tached, tongue-tied, embarrassed, no doubt staring at my shoes. And Sheffield turned out to be a total disaster, as far as I was concerned: no trees to climb, no ponds in which to swim, and above all no Sheila Brunner. There I caught measles and consequently lost most of the sight in my left eye. My sisters were not much company, for they were a good bit older than I—Marjorie by eight years and Sylvia by four. I bumped into them only on rare occasions, standing around the piano trying to sing Gilbert and Sullivan to my mother's inaccurate accompaniment, or hiding under the stairs from the Zeppelins. The sole excitement in my life was the possibility of being bombed by Zeppelins, but Sheffield was a hard place for them to find.

My father had found a war job in Sheffield, making armor plate for battleships. His nights were spent fire watching with a friend from next door, Mr. Rigby. With the guileless candor of a seven-year-old I'm afraid I did not disguise the fact that I would have preferred a father in a glamorous uniform, festooned with decorations for heroic deeds performed "at the front." I suppose that was why I fell in love with my Uncle Vivian.

I had heard dark talk about Uncle Viv. He had been sent to Canada in a great hurry, it was said, and under a fair-sized cloud; I never knew what he had actually done. In the Canadian forces he had become a sniper famous for his accuracy, and he turned up in Sheffield on leave from his regiment roaring drunk and covered with lice. My father propelled him into a Turkish bath to sober him up and, one can only assume, to kill off the lice. He wore a rough khaki uniform, with puttees, and even my father had to admit he was the best shot in the family. Naturally I fell immediately under his spell. I wished my father was a sniper in a tough regiment who would come home on leave full of stories of unbelievable dangers, to say nothing of whisky and lice. It was a far cry from fire watching with Mr. Rigby.

Uncle Viv was the first adult, apart from my mother, to take any real notice of me. I would sit on his knee while he regaled me with stories about Canada and, best of all, bloodthirsty accounts of the war. Apparently the best way he had found to kill Germans was to wait until dawn, hidden in a tree behind the lines; when the enemy came out, half asleep, for their morning toilet, he gave them time to get into a crouching position, took aim, and potted them off. I don't think Uncle Viv bothered much about sportsmanship and sitting ducks; his motto seems to have been "Shoot them when they're stationary, and keep moving yourself!" He always vacated a position the moment he thought the Germans had got a bearing on him—leaving it, alas, to the luckless sniper following on behind him. Needless to say, the losses among the Canadian riflemen were very heavy. But not Uncle Viv: he had learned the hard way, in Canada, how to survive.

He was my hero, and I followed him around like a small dog, until the dreadful day when his leave was over and he returned to the front to catch more Germans unawares. I never saw him again, but I learned that he survived the war, was decorated many times, and became a prosperous timber merchant. Maybe a few more Harrisons should have been packed off to Canada; it might have done some of them a power of good.

After the war, when I was ten, we moved back to Liverpool, settling finally in a district called Sefton Park. It was at about this time that I decided that none of the names I was then called—Reggie, Bobby, Baa—suited me. Somehow I hit on Rex. I must have heard someone calling for their dog and thought it sounded rather nice. My sisters probably disapproved of such a dashing name for their younger brother Reginald, but I stuck to my guns, with the rather reluctant support of my parents, and Rex it became and Rex it has remained.

I soon forgot my mad hero worship for Uncle Viv, as my interest in the opposite sex picked up again in earnest. Cynthia Miles, a blonde who had a lovely bicycle, lived only a few minutes away. I had a bicycle too, and we used to do hair-raising tricks like riding as fast as we could at low branches of trees and hanging on to them, letting the bicycles go on without us until they collapsed in a heap. In those days at least I must have gone for tomboys, though I was well aware that Cynthia was already more shapely than Sheila. I had also begun to notice that my sister Sylvia was growing up and now had boyfriends hanging about, including one called David Maxwell Fyfe, a young Scottish barrister.

At Liverpool College my education, for want of a better word, was completed. My father used to help me with my homework; he was extraordinarily well read. Occasionally we played chess together, though whenever he was leading—which was every time we played—I would, just before the checkmate move, accidentally on purpose upset the board so that the final indignity might not take place.

Two good things happened to me at Liverpool College.

Father with my sister Sylvia and me

With great encouragement from my father I played a lot of cricket and got into the School XI, and I have remained a cricket addict all my life. And I discovered the theatre, taking part in the annual school plays produced by a kind and gentle man called Fred Wilkinson.

I played first in *A Midsummer Night's Dream,* as Flute, the bellows-mender, who doubles as Thisbe, a fair maiden. My mother made me a corn-colored wig that went on like a basin, and a long dress, and I decided to go for an ample bosom and a lisp:

> "O Wall, full often hatht thou heard my moanth
> For parting my fair Pyramuth and me.
> My cherry lipth have often kith'd thy stoneth . . ."

and so on, getting I may say my fair share of laughs. Success obviously went straight to my head and I proceeded to fall in love with the small boy playing Titania, only because he looked so beautifully like a girl. His name, I remember, was Hay Junior, and I followed him everywhere backstage. I should add that my affection did not go beyond the costume, and when he took it off I had no time for him at all. Nor can I remember anybody following me about as Thisbe!

In Maeterlinck's *The Blue Bird* I played the Cat. Apart from my entrance, which I made as big as I could, naturally, with the immortal line *"Mee-ow-you,"* I don't think I had quite as big a success. My mother had muffled me in a sort of velvet suit with a long tail and a hood with ears. The costume got in my way, and I had not yet reached the stage where I could have used the tail to advantage, by tripping over it, or better still, by tripping other people over it. Still I felt rather pleased with myself, and was delighted that Cynthia Miles, as well as my family, had witnessed my triumph.

There was a lot of talk about what I was going to do with my life when I left school. Sylvia's friend David Fyfe was of the opinion that I should become a solicitor. I overheard this, and the idea filled me with icy horror, as indeed did David Fyfe for suggesting it. My mind was made up: I was going to be an actor.

I took my father and mother to one side and confided this to them. I don't think they were unduly surprised. For years I had been making them sit in chairs in the drawing room while I drew the curtains in the bow window and took curtain calls. Apparently I didn't think it necessary to give them any sort of performance, only to appear. Their patience must have been exceptional. In some measure, of course, they had themselves to blame, for taking me a lot to theatres in Liverpool.

After five years at Liverpool College I felt fairly convinced that Einstein had not made a second coming, and that it was time to get on with taking curtain calls, and not in the drawing room. My father very kindly said he would talk to one of the members of the board of the Liverpool Playhouse and see if he could get me an interview with William Armstrong, the resident director.

I was sixteen when I went for that first interview at the Playhouse. William Armstrong, a tall, balding, redheaded Scot, was vague and looked at me with obvious distaste. I'm sure he would have liked me to be prettier; and goodness knows nobody could have accused me of being that. However, he said he would see if he could fit me in as a student at thirty shillings a week. I took a small curtain call and left.

At last, after months of waiting and hoping, the call came—a postcard saying simply, "Please attend rehearsals, 10:30, May 30, 1924." That postcard with "The Playhouse Liverpool" along the top, and signed "William Armstrong," was one of the most exciting things I had ever seen in my life. Naturally I contrived to lose it a day or two later. But I turned up on time on the thirtieth.

A first rehearsal is frightening even now, but to me then, a totally unknown local boy creeping shamefacedly through the stage door and onto a crowded stage, it was a nightmare of embarrassment. Luckily one of the stage managers noticed me and took me over to a bunch of student walk-ons. Gradually I stopped shaking. When at last I could bring myself to look at my seniors they all seemed relaxed; they were casually dressed, and laughing among themselves. They were, as I was to learn, a pretty strong acting group.

The play I had been called to rehearse turned out to be a curtain raiser called *Thirty Minutes in a Street*, by Beatrice Mayor. It was in fact precisely that, a half hour in a street with characters moving on and off stage, so many of them that the company had had to call in recruits. The part that was finally handed to me said, "A distraught father, hair disheveled, runs across the stage shouting, 'Fetch a doctor . . . baby . . .'" This was to be my first utterance on the professional stage.

Although petrified, I managed on that first occasion to rush across saying the line. Nothing happened, no applause, the play went on. In fact nothing happened all through the rehearsals; the members of the company simply saw a young, pimply, gangling local extra filling in.

The first night arrived. I was poised, nervous, ready to give my all—after all, hadn't I succeeded as Thisbe and as the Cat? I ran on and heard myself say, "Fetch a baby . . ." I stopped. I knew that wasn't right. Then in a great flurry of nerves and excitement I shouted, "Fetch . . . a baby doctor." This confusing utterance was naturally received in stony silence.

I stood in the wings utterly demoralized. I knew I could never do it and wondered what had possessed me to try. William Armstrong said nothing. What he thought was another matter, which he was in fact to express very clearly, but at a later date.

I stayed on at the Playhouse two and a half years. Goodness knows how—I can only think my father's influence must have been very powerful. I understudied, played a few little parts, and made some great friends: Basil Moss, a junior member of the Playhouse like myself; Arthur Barbosa, a student at the Liverpool Art School, still one of my closest friends; and Christopher Thomas, who was working at the Leverhulme soap factory and is now a dignified member of the War Office.

We used to sally forth at night to the local dance halls. This was the Roaring Twenties, even in Liverpool. The Adelphi Hotel had opened a spot called the Bear Garden which had an unbelievably noisy band of the washboard variety. They played blues, with a man scraping a piece of wood rhythmically along a wooden washboard—a form of early New Orleans jazz to which Arthur and I were particularly addicted.

Tea dances were the great things, and I remember the crazy flappers with bandanas and short skirts doing the Charleston and Black Bottom. I loved them all—and also my own lovely beige Oxford bags. I was very dressy at this time.

I was not the ardent student that I should have been, but I did watch and learn from productions of Barrie, O'Neill, Galsworthy, Chekhov, Shaw, Ibsen. No Shakespeare that I recall; perhaps it was the dearth of Shakespeare at this time that helped to shape my theatrical upbringing. I got a glow of pride when Hugh Williams thanked me for rolling his umbrella so carefully before handing it to him as he went on the stage; I felt a pang of horror when Robert Speaight, playing Booth in John Drinkwater's play *Abraham Lincoln,* forgot to bring his revolver on in the scene in which he was supposed to shoot Lincoln. In a moment of inspiration he stepped into the box, drew an imaginary knife out of his pocket, and stabbed Lincoln in the back, thus changing history in the most alarming manner. The same actor, Speaight, when playing in a one-act play of Chekhov's called *The Bear,* took off the elaborate beard of which one side had come loose and put it in his pocket without interrupting the speech he was embarked upon.

I had a similar accident when a small part at last came my way. I was cast as a native, Jimmy Kanaka, in a play by

Eugene O'Neill called *Gold.* The thrill of getting that part is still with me: seeing my name on the call-board inside the stage door, not as an understudy or a walk-on but as being *in* the play with the other members of the company, was, to me, like winning the Victoria Cross. The scene I had was with a lot of bearded, rough sailors on a desert island, and I was naked except for a loincloth and a few shark's teeth around my neck. It took some hours to black up my body so that not a spot of white could be seen anywhere, even between my toes. At the center of the stage was a palm tree, which I had to climb during the scene to sight a ship.

It was my big moment. My mother, father, and sisters were out front on the opening night, and as it was the first British production of the O'Neill play, a lot of critics had come from London to see it. But the palm tree was my undoing. Nobody had thought to tell me that it had been fireproofed just before curtain time and was still wet. I went up black and came down almost completely white. I sat cross-legged, trying to expose a piece of myself that was still black to the audience, but alas, without success. I was completely unnerved. Instead of making an exit like a noble savage I slunk off like a whipped cur, still trying to cover the white spots with my arms.

I was also on the stage as a footman in John Galsworthy's play *Old English,* which was Herbert Lomas's great part. I was astonished by the aura that surrounded that wonderful actor, the aroma of cigars and port, and by his absorption in the character. I had to stand behind his chair all through a long scene, and every time he said, "Fill up, fill up . . ." I had to pour him more port. I got so completely lost in his performance that I just stood there, staring at him openmouthed. When he said, "Fill up, fill up . . ." I didn't move, I simply stared. This amazed Lomas as much as the audience, and when he repeated the line there was a huge laugh. He very kindly allowed me to keep the business in. He had a wonderful fruity voice, and I used to go home and amuse my mother and father by giving what I'm now sure was a miserable impersonation of him.

Cast as a messenger with one line in *Abraham Lincoln,* I thought to give some realism to the part even at the first rehearsal and came on stage reeling, completely out of breath. Out of the darkness of the stalls came the voice of William Armstrong: "What's the matter, Harrison, are you ill?"

"No, sir, I am acting," I replied, with as much dignity as I could muster.

I learned to respect the wonderful company that William Armstrong had gathered together in these years. There were two great character actors, James Harcourt and Herbert Lomas, one short and round, the other tall and sardonic. The two juveniles both became famous, Cecil Parker in films and Hugh Williams not only as an actor but as a writer of brilliant stage comedies. The support was very strong in male character actors, but always short on female, until Marjorie Fielding joined the company. She was a stern cardigan-type actress, but extremely accomplished.

The great meeting place for all of us in the Playhouse, and also for the touring companies who came to Liverpool, was the Lyceum Café, a coffeehouse in the middle of the town. I met Carol Reed for the first time there when he was still an actor and had not yet turned to film directing. He was then quite humbly engaged, carrying on a spear in Shakespeare's *Henry VIII* and a pudding in Shaw's *Saint Joan.* In the company with him was an entrancing girl called Primrose Morgan. We used to meet regularly in the Lyceum Café, and one night I plucked up courage to ask her out to supper. I was staggered when she said yes, and after supper said boldly, "Come back to my parents' home for a drink." She said yes. Again I was staggered. Finally she stayed the night, and the following morning I was mildly embarrassed to have to tell my parents that there was an actress called Primrose Morgan staying in the spare room. It was all perfectly innocent, but my father gave me some rather strange looks. He obviously fancied Primrose Morgan too, as indeed who wouldn't?

At one point during my time at the Playhouse, the company went to London for a season. They returned with their ranks depleted by London engagements, and I was taken on as a fully fledged member of the company, with my salary raised to three pounds a week.

During my years with the Liverpool Repertory around fifty plays were done; I appeared in perhaps six of them, in tiny parts, but I learned very little of the art of acting. Many of my contemporaries went to some form of dramatic school and started out with a basic training in the art. I just groped about, blindly at the beginning, without much direction and with little grounding in the English classics. Not that I mind this; had I had the slightest desire at this time to become a classical actor, I would, I am sure, have tried to join Frank Benson and his touring Shakespearean company.

Perhaps training does not make any basic difference, in the long run, to an actor's ability to create a role and hold an audience. But it may help him to realize sooner the seriousness of what he is doing, and to overcome the tension, if not outright fear, a young actor feels confronting an audience.

That feeling of tension can take bizarre forms, even with experienced actors. I remember sitting in the audience at a matinee at the Playhouse and seeing Cecil Parker completely out of control with laughter. He kept waving a handkerchief about, in an absolute paroxysm of mirth. Eventually, leaving the stage for what seemed to be many minutes, he returned gravely—only to lose control again. I could see nothing wrong on the stage, and it seemed to me the most extraordinary behavior, but I was later to find out to my own cost that laughing onstage is a very hard thing to conquer. It has something to do with the forbidden, like laughing in church.

When I came to leave the Playhouse in the hope of getting work in London, William Armstrong begged me, in his very short, precise, Scottish speech, to give up acting. He said the profession was overcrowded and only people with exceptional talent could get to the top. And he said, "Please, Rex, why don't you try and do something else?"

However, I was unshaken in my intention. All right, I thought, I'll never be a successful actor, but I can go on being an unsuccessful actor, nobody can deny me that.

Ironically, in later years William Armstrong claimed to have discovered me.

[CHAPTER TWO]

Touring

Having decided to ignore William Armstrong's advice, I went to London. I felt that somehow I must recapture the thrill I had experienced in school plays, when Thisbe had transported me, and not labor under the handicap of those mournful sidelong Scottish glances of disapproval.

So I embarked on a train from Lime Street Station, with my mother, to go and stay with an Aunt Evelyn Carey near Notting Hill Gate. Aunt Evelyn, who had been married to one of my mother's brothers, was a gay, attractive woman, with an ample figure and a great zest for living. I had met her and her daughters, and felt very cozy in their big flat, which looked over the trees of Leinster Gardens. Among her daughters, Marcella was my favorite, and we had our innocent romantic moments, standing together on the roof of the downstairs maisonette. My mother left me in their warm and splendid care and went back to Liverpool.

It was from Aunt Evelyn's flat that my life started. I had the addresses of a lot of agents dotted about the West End of London, given to me by friends at the Playhouse, Basil Moss and Jack Minster in particular, and I had had cards printed with my name in the middle and "Liverpool Repertory Company" in the corner. Liverpool had a great reputation at this period, and I naturally kept to myself William Armstrong's words of discouragement, so that at the agencies in Charing Cross Road, in Adelphi Terrace, and in St. Martin's Lane, I was allowed through the crowded anterooms filled with every type and size of character extras, who were waiting to be picked out for nonspeaking parts. In those days you didn't have one agent, or at least I didn't; you went to lots of agents, each of whom had odd jobs to hand out, as the managements called around asking for a long tall actor or a short round one, a tough type to play a stable boy or an aristocratic crowd-artist.

At this time, in 1927, the theatres were controlled by actor-managers and their stage managers, and an actor-manager would have his favorites and keep them in his company. Gerald du Maurier at the St. James's and Gladys Cooper at the Playhouse were still holding court.

It was also time for musicals: *Hit the Deck, The Girl Friend* and *The Vagabond King* all came from America, and there were revues like *Clowns in Clover,* farces like Ben Travers' *Cuckoo in the Nest,* with Ralph Lynn and Tom Walls, and even *Dracula.*

There was not much Shakespeare. The Thorndike and Casson revival of *Macbeth,* with Henry Ainley as the Thane, did not last long, though the Old Vic company under the banner of Miss Lilian Baylis went on performing Shakespeare at their temporary home at the Lyric, Hammersmith. A very different picture from today.

The British film industry had only just begun to stir, with Gaumont Films, and then with American quota films—"quota quickies" made over here by American companies, on a budget of one pound per foot of film and never mind the quality, so that they could then unload their Hollywood products on England. The results, naturally, were horrendous, as I saw at first hand when I later played walk-ons in two or three.

All in all, not an easy situation for a spotty provincial boy from Liverpool with no classical training and no entrée to an inner circle, on his first venture into the great exciting London of that time. I suppose I was extremely lucky, because eventually an agent sent me to see Jevan Brandon Thomas, whose father had written *Charley's Aunt*.

I remember going to see him in a rather nice Bloomsbury Square house. He was very cultivated and tall and polite. I liked him—he was easy. He told me that *Charley's Aunt* was to tour England, before the company went to Canada, and said he would contact my agent. I was engaged at twelve pounds a week to play Jack, and we opened in Hull.

We had a very gentlemanly and ladylike cast—ever since Brandon Thomas *père* had written the play and made his fortune out of it, it had become essential in the minds of the Brandon Thomases that the juveniles should be genteel. Charley was played by Michael Shepley, who had just come down from Cambridge. Even on the first night he still needed me to help him with his makeup, a matter of the blind leading the blind. As for the two girls, Joan and Amy, they were so ladylike I can't even remember their names. God, how boring it was, after my ribald Liverpool days. However, I found consolation with barmaids and, naturally, in dance halls. In Whitby I even won a competition as the Best Fox-Trotter on the East Coast, with the barmaid from the Angel.

One of the character actors in the play was James E. Page, who had originated the part of Spettigue. He had played the part for about thirty years, and to mitigate his boredom he spent most of the performance trying to make the younger actors laugh. One of his favorite tricks was to turn his back to the audience and drop his false teeth into his top hat, then turn on us with a beaming toothless smile; there were other unmentionable things that he would appear to be doing into his top hat, as variations on the theme.

I used to find myself helpless with laughter, as I had once seen Cecil Parker on the stage of the Playhouse. Rumors of my behavior got back to London, and Brandon Thomas came, unannounced, to see the show. As luck would have it, he saw

"Juvenile lead"

a good performance—maybe Jimmy Page was having an off night. Even so, Brandon Thomas had a long talk with me about my giddy behavior, saying that I would have to go if it didn't stop. He argued, quite rightly, that audiences are alienated by an actor's laughter if they are not in on the joke.

I was still not fully aware, any more than I had been at the Liverpool Repertory, of the seriousness of the work, although deep down I knew that it was the only thing I wanted to do. I was of course only nineteen and had a very unserious approach to life in general. But by being unserious I was subconsciously learning to relax on stage; my laughter, although infuriating to the audience, helped me to get over my tension. An actor must not be in awe of his audience; the audience must be in awe of him. Whether he is laughing or screaming his head off, he must be their master, or entertainer —whichever way he prefers to view it. An audience can smell a frightened, tensed-up actor the way horses smell fear. And the lights, the sea of faces, the strangeness of it all are such a fearful shock to the budding actor's nervous system that he is apt to find movement extremely difficult. Hands and arms are usually the limbs most afflicted, the hands in particular, and pockets are the salvation—they can also be the deathtrap —of the young actor. Somehow you feel less naked if your hands are tucked away safely in your trousers, and oh, the glory of cigarettes!—anything rather than letting your hands rest comfortably by your side.

In those days if a play was a success in London, a tour went out—sometimes two tours, with a north company and a south company—and so for eight or nine years I toured the provinces, learning to handle different audiences. They varied enormously from one town to the next; a farming community obviously has different values, and a different sense of humor, from a mining community. The south was fairly easy to play to, the north country very hard, and if I learned little else I learned about audience control, which was a beginning, and an important one; a knack that cannot be acquired in the drama schools, which are confined to teaching such things as elocution and fencing.

We lived very well, I must say, while we were touring. We earned anything from seven to ten pounds a week, sometimes more, and we lived in the lodging houses that were always to be found in any town with a theatre. We paid thirty shillings a week for these lodgings, and that also covered our food; we had a bedroom each and shared a sitting room, and the landlady cooked our meals, giving us breakfast and lunch and leaving out something cold for us after the show. The only thing that depressed me in those days was lugging my bags about looking for digs. Sometimes, if we remembered, we would write ahead to the next town to a recommended place.

In those days we touring actors were very much thrown together. We would gather for drinks in the morning, have a large lunch, and then nap before the show. It was a sort of community life that was great fun. We were a little band of people going around the country, a group apart.

We rarely met anyone who lived in the towns we played, but once, when we were in Reading, I had a memorable encounter with one of the locals. It was midsummer, and I hired a canoe; as it was an English midsummer, I was naturally well wrapped up against the cold, in a sweater and thick flannels. I took the canoe out on a wide stretch of the Thames called Caversham Reach, and was paddling along upstream when a motorboat hove in sight, coming downstream at a high rate of knots. I called out to the woman at the helm, but she took no notice of my canoe and roared past, leaving me in a fearsome wake.

Over I went, taking in a lot of water. I came up and looked around for help, but there was none in sight. I struggled for a while to right the canoe by myself, but at last I had to give up and try to swim for the bank. I was by now thoroughly exhausted, and my wet clothes were terribly heavy, but not being a strong swimmer I dared not try to take them off while treading water. When I was within a few yards of the bank, I put my feet down . . . and sank. I was full of water, my feet tangled with the river weeds, and I was down once, down twice . . .

I dimly remember seeing something above my head as I went down for the third time—I suppose I grabbed at it. It was a rake, about six or eight feet long. A park keeper had seen my plight and waded in up to his neck to hold it out to me. He dragged me ashore and administered some rough-and-ready first aid, pumping the river water out of me. I felt like hell, but went on the stage that night. The next day placards appeared advertising the local newspaper, with the headline "ACTOR SAVED BY RAKE." Almost a title for a Restoration comedy.

The average tour lasted about sixteen weeks, and then we would go back to London to look for fresh work. I was now trying to be independent. I actually managed to save twenty or thirty pounds on each tour, and felt therefore that I should not make any further calls on Aunt Evelyn's generosity. I used to stay at a hotel in St. Martin's Lane, a terrible beat-up old place frequented by an odd assortment of people, from which I led a rakish life.

Arthur Barbosa had come to London to study at the Heatherley School of Art, and we used to meet up with friends at Sandy's Bar, near Piccadilly Circus. Sandy's Bar didn't serve drinks, only sandwiches and coffee, and I don't quite know why we all had such an affection for it, except that lots of pretty girls used to congregate there, and it was cheap. I found a friend there called John de Forest, who made me laugh uproariously at his carefree attitude to life. He had nothing to do with the theatre, but had been cut off by his father, the Baron de Forest, and was as broke as I. John and I somehow contrived to catch scabies, and we had to go and lie in hot sulphur baths—a miserable ordeal, but it was the only cure for the ailment then. It entailed a great deal of beer drinking afterward. Eventually John went on to win the British amateur golf championship and was reinstated in his father's good books.

Arthur Barbosa is the only friend who has gone right through my life, as I've gone through his, in success and in failure. Maybe it's because we were born on the same day. There is a sympathetic bond between us which I value very highly. Arthur has had to put up with a lot from me and my moods, which he calls "snake's eyes."

He is of Portuguese extraction, and though he has lived in England all his life, he lives here as if he were in Portugal. He has a lovely great moustache and wears black suits in the sunshine and Panama hats. He is of another era, Arthur—I think he would prefer to have been born in another time and place. He has become a great authority on uniforms, particularly those of the Habsburgs and the Austro-Hungarian Empire. He is a designer and a commercial artist, and had great ability as a painter, but so loathed other people's paintings—almost every picture he saw he despised—that he could not bring himself to concentrate on painting. His remarkable philosophy is to do as little as possible, and to enjoy it as much as possible.

I was never long enough in London to enjoy all its fun and games. After *Charley's Aunt* I got a tour of a play called *Potiphar's Wife,* which had been a success at the Savoy Theatre with Jeanne de Casalis. It was during this play that I developed an interesting phobia. There was a court scene during which I had to sit in the witness-box and say nothing, and each time I played it I grew more convinced that I was going to be sick on the stage and disgrace myself in front of everyone. I came on stage with my pockets full of pills and agonized about my phobia instead of concentrating on the part.

It was on this tour, however, that I met Christine Barry, a

With Arthur Barbosa

very pretty young actress, and fell in love with her, and took her back to meet the family. We became inseparable and did several tours together. Christine was the adopted daughter of a couple called Hancock, who lived at Barry in South Wales— hence her choice of a stage name. Her real mother was said to have been a very handsome woman, dangerously fond of pear cider, and her father a blue-blooded lord. Christine herself had great bearing and superb manners. She was unique in that she had been born with white hair. It was a source of embarrassment to her, so she dyed it, but I found it irresistible —terribly pretty in so young a girl.

In the end, alas, we parted. It looked as though I was going to go on muddling through in the provinces, enjoying my beer, my digestive biscuits and double Gloucester cheese, and Christine was eager to get to London. The redoubtable Seymour Hicks, who had knocked me off my seat with laughter when my parents took me to see him play years before in Liverpool, took a fancy to her and to my deep distress took her under his voluminous wing.

To get my mind off my misery, I bought a car. It cost, I think, twelve pounds ten, and it was called an Airedale. I've never come across an Airedale since, but it had a twelve-horsepower engine, a custom-built body, and an airedale dog on the front of the hood. I didn't know how to drive it, but things were a bit more lax in those days. Kind friends told me what to do: "Let the clutch out, very slowly, press the accelerator, let the brake off, and Bob's your uncle."

I got into my car and only then realized it was standing on a slope. This presented me with a further problem, a question of timing. The car and I persisted in going backward, a menace to pedestrians and everything else around. Eventually I persuaded the Airedale to chug up the hill, far enough to turn into a level street, and gradually, after some hair-raising experiments, taught myself to drive. For some time afterward I must have been a terrible road hazard, as my mind was more on my lost love than on the Airedale. My family came to see me while we were in Bournemouth, and I surprised them with my new car; they duly admired it, which made me feel better.

After *Potiphar's Wife* I went on to do a series of plays, *The Chinese Bungalow, Cup of Kindness,* and others, none of which would mean much to anybody today, though they were all successes in their time. We had problems with *The Chinese Bungalow*. We were playing the music halls in the suburbs of London, where for some reason the audiences didn't warm to the Chinese. The English actor playing the leading Chinese part had to march down to the audience more than once and tell them to shut up, before resuming his Chinese posture, hands in sleeves, and his "chelly blossom" accent.

We often had to go on with a show while fights were in progress in the auditorium, particularly in the north country. We would hear someone in the gallery take a great crack on the jaw, and an outburst of groans and shouts, all of which we had to ignore. Sometimes there was a hum of chatter and whispering, and I once threw myself completely by turning around to shush the audience and then being at a loss for my next line. It takes years to develop ways of thrilling or subduing an audience, and to learn, when you've got a very tough audience on your hands, not to give up. You have to stand up to them.

Another role I had on tour was in John Van Druten's *After All,* which had been well received in London. Years later I got to know Van Druten well, when I starred in his play *Bell, Book and Candle* and worked over the script with him to anglicize it before it was put on in London. *After All* went out on tour with the director who had staged it in London, a close friend of Van Druten's. Rehearsals went very well, as far as I was concerned, until I overheard the director confiding to someone, "Rex is really far too normal to get on." I puzzled about this. I didn't think being normal was all that bad. In fact I was enjoying being normal, enormously.

In 1934 I went through a very lean period in London, living in a bed-sitting room in Lancaster Gate. I was asked if I would play three or four little parts in *Richard III,* which Baliol Holloway was performing at the Prince of Wales Theatre, now a musical-comedy house. Well, I'd do anything in those days.

It was my first and last appearance in Shakespeare. In one of my roles I had to answer the question "What is't o'clock?" with "Upon the stroke of four," and the story went around that before giving this answer I lifted my chain mail to look at my watch. Quite untrue, of course. But I gave the line in such a naturalistic manner that it was taken away from me and given to Bernard Miles—Sir Bernard now, who runs the Mermaid Theatre.

Another of my little speeches came in the battle scene, when Richmond turns and asks, "Where is Lord Stanley quarter'd, dost thou know?" The reply is, "His regiment lies half a mile at least/South from the mighty power of the king." I found this an absolute tongue twister. I said it to myself over and over. On opening night I started out, "His regiment lies . . . south? . . . east," lost my head, and went on, ". . . the mighty power of the king of France." The king of France, of course, has no business at all in *Richard III,* so my version of the line caused a certain consternation. Baliol Holloway came down to the wings to watch, the second night, hoping I'd do it again, but I had taken such fright that I managed to get lost amid the scenery during one of the changes and simply didn't show up. Richmond saw I wasn't there and smoothed over the question. The third night I screwed up my courage and delivered that epic line successfully.

After this notable success, I appeared at the same theatre in a play called *The Ninth Man,* a thriller. I had quite a nice little part in which I invented all sorts of business and indulged in my favorite eccentricities. James Agate, the critic, reviewed the performance and finished up his notice by saying, "The actor, whose name escapes me, did something more by bringing a new method, a new style of entertaining us." I never forgave Agate for allowing my name to escape him.

With a friend called Tom Macaulay I took a flat in Shepherd Market. It was in Hertford Court and consisted of two bedrooms and a sitting room, a small bathroom, an even smaller kitchen. It was fun, but it did not make any special improvement in my fortunes. Work was becoming harder to find. The talking pictures had arrived from America—Warner Brothers started it all, with Al Jolson in *The Jazz Singer*— and a great many of the theatres in the provinces at which the touring companies had played were being converted into movie houses. I was often at a loose end and spent a lot of my time at various parties in the neighborhood.

It was at one of these parties that I met my first wife, Collette. One night when I had been stood up by a girl, I rang the telephone number Collette had given me and invited her for a drink. Her name wasn't really Collette, but Marjorie; she had changed it, she told me, in her late teens, because she did not feel like a Marjorie. When I told her that one of my sisters was called Marjorie, Collette said this had no bearing on her case.

We began to see quite a lot of each other, and eventually I was asked down to meet her family. They lived in a pretty house called The White House, at Stratton, a small village near Bude in Cornwall. Collette's father, Major Thomas, was a retired officer, a nice, shy man who allowed his wife Jessie to rule the roost.

When Collette presented me, a starving actor living in a room in Shepherd Market, Jessie was horrified. "Can't you get a *job?*" she asked reprovingly. She was immensely ambitious for her daughters. The announcement that we intended to get married threw Jessie into a veritable tizzy. The

With Collette at the premiere of *Marie Antoinette*

Major prudently disappeared into the garden, as he always did when Jessie got worked up. It must have been some consolation to my ex-mother-in-law when, some time after Collette and I were married, her second daughter, Jane, fell in love with and married the Duke of Somerset.

Our marriage was stormy: we were young, I was poor, Collette was pregnant. We lived in a little flat Collette had found in Bruton Mews. We used to buy a pint at the local and take it home to drink with dinner—Collette was quite a good cook. The big end had gone on my Airedale, and I borrowed twenty pounds from my mother to buy another car, a Chrysler. The mechanic who sold it to me ran a repair shop in the garage beneath our flat, and when our son, Noel, was born, he spent many hours in his baby carriage, amid the gasoline fumes of the Mews, watching the mechanic perform major and expensive operations on the Chrysler.

Like many of my early cars the Chrysler had a knack for getting me into awkward spots. Sometime later I was in a play with Hugh Wakefield, a fine comedian who had a sporting air and wore an eyeglass, and he invited me to drive down

into the New Forest, where Constance, Duchess of Westminster had a house, for the weekend. We proposed to go
each in his own car, but I particularly asked Wakefield to
drive slowly once we were in the New Forest so that I could
stay right behind him and use his headlights. I dared not use
mine: as soon as the Chrysler's headlights were switched on,
everything blew out.

Not altogether surprisingly, Wakefield soon forgot this request and picked up speed. I could not go as fast as he, and
with my sidelights could see nothing. I switched on the headlights and everything went black. Before I knew it I was off
the road and into a pond, and there I sat, axle-deep in water,
mourning my suitcase, which had gone through the windshield.
It was some time before Wakefield came back and found me,
and the suitcase, which was more pondweed than suits, and
bore me off to a very grand house, full of very grand footmen.
The next day we went back with a horse called Blossom and
yanked the car out of the pond, and afterward I wrote up the
incident in a piece for *Lilliput,* getting my own back on
Wakefield and on the Chrysler.

Meanwhile I went on touring in the wilderness. I was in
Nottingham, in a particularly undistinguished play called
The Wicked Flee, when I was summoned to attend rehearsals,
on trial, of Robert Morley's first play, *Short Story*. I thought
I was having delusions of grandeur. *Short Story* was a comedy
with a very distinguished cast indeed, headed by Dame Marie
Tempest, A. E. Matthews, and Dame Sybil Thorndike, and
supported by Margaret Rutherford, Isabel Jeans, Graham
Browne, and, I hoped, myself. The director was that true
genius of the theatre, Tyrone Guthrie.

At the first reading, at His Majesty's Theatre, A. E. Matthews arrived on a bicycle, trundled it down the steps on to
the stage, and propped it against the back wall. He was a
strange sight, wearing riding breeches and a Norfolk jacket.
He and Tyrone Guthrie and the rest of the cast sat around

a table, while I hovered in the background, unwilling to attract the attention of those great giants of the theatre, as we waited for Dame Marie Tempest to make her entrance.

And what an entrance it was. Dame Marie was a small, very straight-backed woman with enormous elegance and charm, and a fearsome reputation as a martinet. All sorts of stories circulated about her; it was rumored that she used to have her chair nailed to the floor, upstage center, so that nobody could move it and destroy her commanding position over the players. Her entrance that day, down the steps and onto the stage, was a triumph. She was in gray, with a very elegant long umbrella which she carried at arm's length, adding a further dimension of stateliness to her manner. For a chap from *The Wicked Flee* it was a revelation.

Much to my amazement I was taken on, to play the part of a middle-aged American producer. When I asked Hugh Beaumont, the manager of H. M. Tennent, why, he said they had worked out the average age of the cast and found it was over seventy; they thought a younger actor would bring the average down a little. "Binkie" Beaumont and I were firm friends from then on. From his office over the Globe Theatre in Shaftesbury Avenue he for many years virtually controlled the London theatre, and he played a considerable part in my career. He was one of the best producers I have met, calm, methodical, a genius with people.

So, early each morning, I took the train from Nottingham to attend rehearsals, returning every afternoon to my wretched *Wicked Flee*. I watched, wondered, admired, and learned from Tyrone Guthrie and the great stars, and particularly from A. E. Matthews. I watched him not only at rehearsals but, when we opened, from the side of the stage every night. He had an unbelievably subtle way of disguising his comic effects, trying for new ones and discarding the old.

We opened out of town, in Glasgow, and then came to London. It fascinated me to see Dame Marie, on opening nights, shaking with nerves to such an extent that, during the tea party which seemed always to feature in her plays, her teacup had to be glued to the saucer.

I had a short scene with Dame Marie, after which we left the stage together through the inevitable french windows of that period. Almost before we were out of sight of the audience, Dame Marie started to clap her hands loudly; whereupon the audience, thinking that the noise came from some enthusiast in their midst, took up the clapping. I looked sidelong at Dame Marie, thinking it was a joke, but not at all —she was quite serious, and it happened at every performance.

Her curtain calls, too, were masterfully handled. After the routine cast calls, she appeared by herself and then most graciously brought on Sybil Thorndike from one side and Matthews from the other. By that time the applause was dying down, but still the curtain went up, and a maid planted in the wings would catapult onto the stage Dame Marie's little Sealyham dog. The audience adored it. Dame Marie made a great pantomime of shooing the dog away, and wondering how he could have followed her onto the stage, and then finally would take the trembling, unwilling creature into her arms and hug it, and get two more curtain calls all to herself.

I think it was the day after the opening in Glasgow, as we were all having a prelunch drink at the Central Hotel, when Guthrie turned to me and said, "How would you like to go to America?" I stared at him: I was unaccustomed to moving in this sort of society. He went on to explain that he was directing a play over there called *Sweet Aloes,* in which there was a good part for me.

I gulped down my drink and said, "That would be lovely."

Lovely indeed it was, for me. Hugh Beaumont arranged for me to be released from *Short Story* and helped me to get two transatlantic passages. Collette was not so keen. She had fallen in love—not with me, I hasten to say, but with another supporting actor of the day. However, we sent Noel down to

Cornwall to stay with the formidable Jessie, Collette had a tearful farewell with her friend, and we set off on board the *Majestic*. Collette stayed only until the opening in New York, then returned—to join her son, she said.

New York in 1936 was very different from today. The town never slept, Harlem was warm and welcoming, and the big nightclubs with all the great bands of that period were in full swing. The blues had come up from the Deep South and changed to jazz, moved from New Orleans to Chicago to New York; and jazz was at its peak, with Paul Whiteman and Benny Goodman, Count Basie, Fats Waller, Jack Teagarden, Louis Armstrong.

Much later, in the Fifties, I did a television program for CBS called *Crescendo*, in which I played an Englishman arriving in the States for the first time and being shown around, and I actually did a number with Satchmo, called "That's Jazz." I am not notoriously unmusical, but Armstrong was so worried for me he held my arm and pinched it to the rhythm. It was a sweet gesture.

In 1936 my rehearsal money was about sixty dollars a week, and I lived on a diet of milk and baked potatoes and had to borrow money—from the author of the play, Joyce Cary to pay for my hotel room. I developed a new phobia, that I was going to jump out of the window. I had difficulty with heights anyway, so I used to ask for a room on a lower floor, which was noisier but cheaper than one with a view. I think my phobia was sheer nervous agitation; New York could be very frightening for an untraveled young actor, and I, who had never been out of England before, was scared and hungry.

My leading lady was the much-loved Evelyn Laye, a very popular singing star who had never done a straight play before. She was married to Frank Lawton, who had made a number of films in Hollywood, and they had what seemed to me a very luxurious apartment, where Evelyn practiced on me her theories about relaxation. I had to lie on the floor, flat out, and relax from my toes right up through my knees,

45

my back, my neck, and finally open my mouth wide and let my jaw go slack; then start on my arms and go right down to my fingers. Before I knew it I would be sound asleep on the floor, and more than once I woke up to find Evelyn's husband gazing down at me. I just gave him a beatific smile —luckily he was a friend.

The stagehands went on strike during our rehearsal period, and I have a vivid picture in my mind of Tyrone Guthrie pushing a large handcart full of props from the theatre, where we were not allowed to rehearse, up Seventh Avenue to a hired hall. But when we opened, the critics were not kind. Robert Benchley, writing in *The New Yorker,* gave me a good review, which was a great boost to my morale, but called the play "Sweet Alousy," and commented that "this might be all right for a foggy day in London, but it does not suit a bright Manhattan one." Off we came, within three weeks.

I returned home on the *Aquitania,* together with Joyce Cary, who was a great and kindly companion. I was met, not by Collette, but by my mother, and started trying to pick up the threads.

CHAPTER THREE

London Without Tears

Even in those days news got around, and though *Sweet Aloes* had not had a success in New York, it got back that I had had a few good reviews.

But before the next offer came along, I spent some days at the flat in Bruton Mews—not happy days. Collette was working in a hat shop run by fancy male designers and very often didn't come home till quite late at night. We had Noel back with us again, and I used to enjoy watching him stagger about in his long nightdress, taking, as all children do, some incredible falls without harm or complaint. As Collette was out so much, we had an Irish daily girl in to take care of Noel. Once while I was sitting watching him being bathed by this girl I rather foolishly asked her what she would do if she won the Irish Sweepstakes. She said with great venom, "I'd never see another baby as long as I lived." I reported this to Collette and the girl was sacked.

Eventually I got a phone call from the St. Martin's Theatre, where I had played a small part, before going to America, in a play called *The Man from Yesterday*, with Leslie Banks. They asked if I would go and see them about another play they were going to present. God, what a relief—both financially and emotionally.

It was called *Heroes Don't Care,* and it was an extremely funny play about the frailties of polar explorers, written by two little old ladies who lived in Australia. I was asked to play the part of Tom Gregory, who was the antihero, perhaps one of the first of that now common breed. He gets cold feet in Narvik, the last civilized stop in Norway before the big push up to the Pole. He is so frightened he decides to hold up the expedition by seducing the leader's wife. Chaos ensues, and in the aftermath of the seduction the expedition is all but forgotten. The leader, Sir Edward Pakenham, is a brave, methodical, middle-aged man, played most beautifully by Felix Aylmer, and such a blimp that the audience saw his sexual troubles as just deserts and took the antihero's side. An interesting reaction in 1936, when heroes were still accepted very much as heroes. One could not imagine anyone twenty-five years earlier poking fun at a Captain Scott, and although this play was written before the Second World War it may have been a pointer toward things to come.

It ran for seven months, and on the strength of this performance I won a very lucrative contract with Alexander Korda. He offered me 2,500 pounds a year, which to me seemed—and was—a fortune, in return for which I would make films at his studios, while he was free to loan me out and reimburse himself from any earnings I might make in the theatre or in other studios. It wasn't, for Korda, too large a gamble; for me it meant a guaranteed income, a marvelous relief at that time. I felt that now perhaps I could withstand the pressures on my marriage and make it work. After all, I had Noel to think of, who was a real joy to me.

We moved into a bigger flat in Sloane Street and found a proper nanny for Noel—not from Ireland this time, but from Bedford, which I thought might be safer. Still I found myself forever in debt, and in the end had to put the housekeeping into the hands of my agent, Vere Barker. Somehow we staggered on.

I began, though, to throw off the woes and frights of New York and found that I no longer needed relaxing exercises. I started to expand, and my night life sparkled—so did my acting, except on matinee days. No more hanging around Sandy's Bar, hoping for work and just looking at the pretty girls; now came night life of a less arduous nature, at Millie Howie's Bag o' Nails, Ma Meyrick's Forty-Three Club, Rosa Lewis's Cavendish Hotel, wonderful warm haunts of adventure and entertaining chat. Wandering with friends through the streets from coffee stall to coffee stall, I saw the London of the late Thirties in full swing—not like the latter-day Carnaby Street, but swinging nevertheless. There was just as much going on as today, only then it did not pay to advertise. As Mrs. Patrick Campbell said, it didn't matter what you did, "as long as you don't do it in the street and frighten the horses."

Alexander Korda, the head of Denham Studios, was a miracle man, a great figure. He worked immensely hard and ran the studio beautifully, while in London leading a life of ease and comfort with an enormous circle of friends. He was also extremely well read. When I was a young man he alarmed me slightly: he had such a big personality that one felt a dwarf beside him. But when he was talking to you you immediately felt that there was no one else in the world he wanted to talk to—you were the center of his universe. He had an irresistible way with him and could charm the hind legs off a donkey—the hind legs belonging, in the main, to the Prudential Insurance Company, which financed him. His plans were invariably expansive and ambitious, and he kept the British film industry at a higher peak for a longer time than anyone else has ever done, including Rank. He imported stars from America and Europe, he imported cameramen, he had a great designer in his brother Vincent Korda, who did the sets, and another director in Zoltan Korda—they were three remarkable Hungarian brothers.

My contract started with a small part, as a reporter, in *Men Are Not Gods,* with that marvelous actress Miriam Hopkins. I remember, while I was still totally unversed in the art of film acting and scared like hell of the camera, watching Miriam doing a silent scene, standing at a window and just turning on the tears. I thought it was miraculous.

Apart from the few bits I had done in the "quota quickies" to make an honest penny in the very early days, I had no film experience whatsoever, and a camera, even a home-movie camera, is a profoundly unnerving object. Nearly everybody goes rigid in front of even a Kodak. The trick, for turning on tears as for everything else, is to relax absolutely. If you don't you can't do anything. It takes a long time to learn to treat the camera as a friend and confidant, which finally you have to do if you're to become a good film actor. On the set you can actually hear the film going through the camera, very indistinctly but you can just hear it, and that, when you are relaxed, is the moment when you start to think, acting for the camera and for nobody else. The director is there to be your eyes and to say, "No, do it again, that wasn't quite what we want," or, "I don't think that's quite as you'd like it." But you don't think about the director when you're acting, you think only of that audience, that camera lens.

My next film was with Vivien Leigh, a lighthearted comedy called *Storm in a Teacup,* based on a farce by James Bridie, which he had adapted from the German of Bruno Frank. It was about a young journalist setting a small town in Scotland about its ears with his exposé of a local magistrate's heavy-handed justice. The *Spectator* commented: "Here, at last, is a reasonable humanity presented with humour and understanding. It is certainly the first genuinely British comedy to appear from an English studio."

Vivien Leigh had reached a difficult and fascinating point

in her life. She was still married to Leigh Holman, who was a highly successful barrister, and she and Olivier had just done a film together called *Fire over England*. I remember that Vivien hoped to go to Elsinore to play Ophelia in *Hamlet*, opposite Olivier, and when she feared she couldn't, she broke down in the dressing room in wild hysteria, anger, and anguish. She was very like a cat. She would purr and she would scratch, and she looked divinely pretty doing either. Driving home from the studios with Vivien after work, I remember feeling a total worm once more, as if I had gone back to the days of Sheila Brunner—totally unable to express myself, and with Vivien, alas, no chance of swimming in a pond among the tadpoles. All she wanted to do was to talk about Larry, and so I went along with that, gazing on that beautiful face with unhopeful ardor. I loved Vivien. Although we never as much as held hands, I cannot say my love was platonic; it was more exciting than that. After she married Larry we all became great friends, and many happy and hilarious weekends were spent with them at Notley Abbey and at their house in Chelsea.

Storm in a Teacup was directed by Victor Saville, who was a lot of fun, and the director who started to relax me. In *Men Are Not Gods* I had been directed by a very intense German called Walter Reich; Victor was untense, and his very presence helped me to relax. He was an exceptionally easy, large, jolly man, and he made you uncare, so that you started to unwind, to speak the lines casually and naturally, and to think for the camera. It was really Victor, whom I've seen a lot of since, off the golf course and on, who started me out, and not by saying anything, simply by being himself.

Now I had a tremendous break, for I was offered the leading part in *French Without Tears*. This was Terence Rattigan's second play and his first major success. It was beautifully made and very funny and human, and it became a household word and the toast of the town—a vogue, if you like, attended

French Without Tears: (left to right) Guy Middleton, Trevor Howard, Leueen McGrath, R.H., Robert Flemyng, Kay Hammond, Roland Culver, Percy Walsh (Angus McBean)

in droves by royalty, by the nobility and the café society of the day. Many people came five or six times to see it, when they could get in.

The owner of the Criterion Theatre, Bronson Albery, did not originally have much faith in *French Without Tears*. It was put on in the first place as a stopgap, and we didn't go out on tour. After the dress rehearsal the three partners who'd put up the money sat around wondering how they were going to survive. If I'd had a hundred pounds that evening, I could have bought a third share of that play; one of the partners was very anxious to unload his share—because he couldn't, he made a fortune.

Terry Rattigan remains to this day one of my nearest and dearest friends. He is, as the Irish would say, "a lovely fellow," and apart from being an enormously cultivated person is one of the most brilliant playwrights of our generation. He had a great start in life, at Harrow, where he distinguished himself as a cricketer, and at Trinity College, Oxford, where he was a Modern History Scholar. His father, Frank Rattigan, was a diplomat and a very dashing figure. During the run of *French Without Tears* he appeared on most nights in a box at the Criterion with a young girl on his arm, to show off his son's play and, one presumed, himself too, for he was a very handsome man. Terry's mother was even more beautiful, a red-headed Irishwoman of tremendous spirit, interested in all things, new and old. I will never forget her in her later years, her vitality was still so vivid; she was known affectionately as "Old Blighty," though I never asked Terry why.

Terry of course went on to bigger and greater things, as indeed did many members of that young cast—Kay Hammond, Roland Culver, Robert Flemyng, Trevor Howard. It was then, too, that I met Harold French, who directed *French Without Tears*, and with whom I subsequently did Noël Coward's *Design for Living* and S. N. Behrman's *No Time for Comedy*. We became great chums and still are. Harold had already had a long career in the theatre, having gone on

the stage when he was only twelve, and had many successes
as an actor before turning to directing, on both stage and film.
Lately he has become a writer, and a damn good one too, as
anyone will agree who has read his reminiscences of the
theatre.

I suppose my own life then was so full of goodies that I
had no time to realize that my marriage to Collette was slipping fast. Korda had leased me out to do the play but had
exacted from the management that I should not play matinees
on days when he was using me as well, in films. For two solid
years I played every night at the theatre and worked every day
in the film studios. It meant being called at six o'clock in
the morning and driving down to the studios, working there
until about half past five, going back to the flat in Sloane
Street for a quick meal, and on again to the Criterion, where
we finished at about eleven. I don't know how I did it. I'd
hate to do it now.

The second film I made with Vivien Leigh was also with
Charles Laughton, who, together with the German Erich
Pommer, had his own producing company. It was called *St.
Martin's Lane,* and was written by Clemence Dane. Retitled
Sidewalks of London in America, it was about buskers, the
people who entertained the queues outside theatres, a rum
collection of vaudevillians and straight entertainers who have
disappeared now—along with the theatre queues.

Charles Laughton was a most interesting and eccentric
chap. While he was making *St. Martin's Lane* he lived in a
tree—a tree house, out in the woods. He used to come to work
with bunches of wild flowers that he had picked on his "door-
step"; his huge hands carrying those delicate little flowers I
shall always remember. It could be very awkward acting with
him, because he was so large physically that it was quite difficult to get yourself anywhere near the camera. His bulk
seemed to fill the screen. He was a stage actor originally but
then began to concentrate on films. He could do things in
front of the camera totally without shame, without any sense

of embarrassment, and therefore, of course, became a very great screen actor.

It was during the shooting of my next film, *Over the Moon,* with Merle Oberon, that I began to flag. It went on for seventeen weeks, which in those days was a very long time for a film. The script was based on a story by the American author Robert Sherwood, who I think must have had his mind on higher things while writing it.

New Year's Day came around while I was on this taxing film, and it was a matinee day. I'd had rather a late night on New Year's Eve, to say the least, and was on call for the studio. But the call never came, and I, thinking that they wouldn't really be expecting me at the theatre, decided that I had better go and have a Turkish bath. I had a man-eating hangover and hoped to get myself right for the evening show. I came out of the Turkish bath feeling slightly better and went down to give my evening performance—to be told at the stage door that there were instructions from Mr. Bronson Albery not to allow me in the theatre.

It was a dreadful shock. I realized they had been expecting me for the matinee and had known I was not at the studio, and I was convinced that they had sacked me. I called my agent and told him I'd been barred from the theatre. He came down and we had a large drink together, and decided I could only call up Bronson Albery and ask if I might go down and see him in the country the next day, Sunday.

Albery was a kindly man, and he sent a message to say he'd see me the following afternoon. I drove down, miles into the country, and was shown into the study, where I waited, like a small schoolboy. Albery gave me a good dressing down, in full headmaster style, and then reinstated me. I had a cup of tea with the family after that, and they were quite amiable. I had been thinking it was the end of my career, and all for the sake of a Turkish bath.

I had done one other film, *The Citadel,* adapted from the best-selling novel by A. J. Cronin, a doctor turned writer.

Robert Donat played the hero, an honest country doctor, with Rosalind Russell as his co-star, while I played a young Harley Street specialist living off the rich hypochondriacs of Belgravia. In one scene I came out of a private room in a very luxurious clinic and, upon being asked by a fellow doctor how my patient's chest was doing, answered gleefully, "It's a treasure chest." All the doctors in Harley Street got the joke, and I couldn't go to see a doctor in those days without their bringing it up.

I was myself a giant hypochondriac at this time, so my visits to specialists, when I could afford them, were not infrequent. One occasion I remember particularly, when I had gone for a totally unnecessary examination of my intestines. The procedure was to blow you up with air, X-ray you, and show you smartly to the door with a "Good-bye, you're fine." I climbed happily into a taxi to go and see a rehearsal of the American company of *French Without Tears,* which was to open shortly in New York. I was still blown up like a balloon, and I let the air out as slowly as I could, to no avail: the taxi driver turned around to ask if he was going too fast for me. I tried to reassure him, and we made it to the theatre, but there, in the stalls, the real trouble started. The English actors going off to America thought I must be commenting on their performances. Finally I had to slink off to relieve myself, only to return to find the detonations went on, even louder. I don't think Frank Lawton, who was playing my part, ever felt the same about me again.

By now I had had two years of filming and stage acting at one and the same time. I really was exhausted, and as *French Without Tears* was transferring from the Criterion to the Piccadilly Theatre, I asked the management for a release. A replacement was found, and I went away for four weeks' rest.

It was the summer of 1938. Despite great rumors of war Collette and I set out for the South of France with Harold French and his wife, Phyl, who was later tragically killed in the blitz. We enjoyed ourselves at St. Tropez until we were informed that war was about to be declared: all English people were to leave France immediately.

The drive back was exceptionally unpleasant. I had a Brough Superior sports car then—I seem to have gone in for onetime cars, like the Airedale and the Brough, which no one else has ever heard of—and it didn't behave at all well. Eventually it went off the road and ran into a bank, and when I backed it off and started again I discovered that it was boiling over. I got out to investigate the radiator, which had a rather racy swivel cap, and got a jet of blinding, boiling water in my face.

By the time they got me to Paris I was practically unconscious and looked like Lon Chaney in his greatest disguise. I had bad burns, and for a while was attended daily by doctors. The pain was indescribable, and my face was completely wrapped up, except for two slits for my eyes and another for my mouth. I was lucky though, because I had been very tanned and this helped to keep the skin intact; I had no scars.

I lay in bed at the Crillon for ten days, and all I could hear on the radio was Hitler's ranting and raving. Except for Charleys like me who couldn't be moved, all the English had been sent home, and Harold had had to go on, leaving me behind. When I was allowed up and started walking around Paris with my bandages still on, people called out, *"O mon brave!"* as though they took me for a casualty of the war as yet undeclared. I got home finally, minus bandages and tan, at about the same time as Chamberlain got back with his umbrella, his piece of paper, and his "peace in our time." Being extremely cowardly, and totally unversed in politics, I was of course absolutely delighted by his pronouncement: my ears were still ringing from Hitler's filthy shouting at Nuremberg.

I was then asked to play in Noël Coward's *Design for Living*, with Diana Wynyard as my leading lady, at the Haymarket, which was, and still is, my favorite theatre in the

Design for Living: R.H., Anton Walbrook, Diana Wynyard
(Angus McBean)

world. *Design for Living* had been done in America with Lynn
Fontanne and Alfred Lunt, and with Noël Coward himself
in the part that I now played. Directed by Harold French, it
had a very considerable success in London, as in America, and
ran for a year.

Diana I grew very fond of—I did another play with her
afterward, which is always a sign of friendship. She was a
bit of a sergeant-major, in the nicest possible way, a very
pretty sergeant-major. When I was off for a week with an
inner-ear infection she used to telephone regularly and shout
at me, "Rex—get up!" which did nothing to aid my recovery.
Anton Walbrook, who was also in the play, was a gentle
man with a rather heavy *Götterdämmerung* personality, not
in my opinion God's gift to the comedy stage. I was going

through a have-to-have-jazz phase, and whenever I was off I played New Orleans jazz flat out in my dressing room. Anton, poor man, was next door, and I used to hear his groans even over the uproar of my machine. If only I had liked Bach, or Beethoven . . .

I had an unnerving experience at one matinee. I had a very quick change, from tailcoat into pajamas, and I was in the middle of it when I got a call from nature. I came back on-stage all right, so I thought, and stood, looking as unflappable as ever, next to Walbrook, until I realized that people were staring at me in amazement. When I glanced down I found that my pajama bottoms were on the wrong way around; the seat was hanging down the front, and everybody was convinced I'd done it for a gag. They were speechless with laughter—I was not amused.

CHAPTER FOUR

Major Barbara and Flight-Lieutenant Harrison

T HE fourth of September, 1939, the morning after war was declared, found me sitting in my flat alone and disconsolate. *Design for Living* had been playing to capacity when the theatres closed down. I was appalled by the thought of no performance to do that night, worrying about how to cope with the blackout and what I ought to do next. I had nobody to discuss this with. Noel had been sent down to his grand-parents in Cornwall for safekeeping, and Collette had left to join the Red Cross. She was to go for training somewhere out-side London. This is how far apart we had grown—and I hardly ever saw her again. I suppose we both knew it was no go.

My friends were all extremely apprehensive, and I person-ally felt that the skies were going to open at any minute and rain down fire, liquid gas, and germs, all at the same time. I was deeply preoccupied with these terrifying pictures of destruction when the phone rang, almost giving me a heart attack. It was Vere Barker, my redoubtable agent—Major Vere Barker, to be exact, for it turned out that he was an officer in the reserve. In very military tones he said, "I am holding a place for you, Rex, in the Inns of Court Cavalry Regiment.

Get into a taxi right away and get down there and see the colonel."

I said, "Wait a minute—I thought you were my theatrical agent, not a recruiting officer."

"It's a damn fine regiment," said Major Vere Barker, and the line went dead.

I stood for a while, staring across Sloane Street, then kissed myself good-bye and set off for the Inns of Court. There I met the colonel of the regiment, a charming man who took down my particulars. He said they were not taking any more recruits at the moment, but that I would receive my call-up papers as soon as I was needed. I thanked him and left, feeling rather as if I had auditioned for a part that I was not quite sure I wanted. But I had taken my first step for king and country, so I called Vere Barker to tell him the outcome of my meeting with the colonel. Then, rather than sit alone in the flat in Sloane Street, waiting to be called up, I went to stay with a cousin of mine, Bat Tonge, and her husband, Buster, at Rudlow Manor, near Bath.

The countryside was looking its best, and so was the manor house; the days went by uneventfully, playing croquet, eating, chatting, and sleeping. Bat and Buster too were exercised as to what Buster should do next. Occasionally we went for a walk and I watched Buster shooting rabbits. It was all very unlike my usual existence, but then I was in limbo, expecting every day to have my call-up papers forwarded to me.

Nothing happened. Vere Barker on the telephone said he had heard that my papers had gone to me, but when I got in touch with the Inns of Court again it transpired that they had gone astray. Meanwhile all the places in the regiment had been filled. If I had managed to get into it, it is unlikely that Vere Barker would have seen any more of his 10 percent commission on my theatrical earnings. Few, if any, of the original members of that regiment survived the war.

In early October, Hugh Beaumont traced me to Rudlow Manor and rescued me, as he had rescued me once from Nottingham. He called to suggest that we should do something about the theatre. The blood began to race again through my veins, I thanked Bat and Buster most profusely for having been so sweet and protective of me, jumped into my car, and tore back to London.

Hugh had been looking into the situation and had found that because we were at war the provincial theatres were willing to consider cooperative arrangements, whereby they took some 30 percent of the box-office receipts and let the touring company take 70 percent. And so Diana Wynyard, Anton Walbrook, and I decided to take to the road with *Design for Living*. It was risky, because we did not know whether people would come out of their homes in the blackout, but as it happened we did an extremely successful tour. It was still the period of what was called the phony war, and the audiences flocked to the theatres. They were starving for entertainment.

Our engagement in Birmingham coincided with the appearance at a rival theatre of *You, of All People,* in which Leslie Banks was playing, with Lilli Palmer. I knew Leslie quite well and of course he introduced me to Lilli. As her play and mine were both scheduled for Liverpool the following week, I offered to drive her up there in my car, a secondhand Bentley for which I had exchanged the lethal Brough Superior.

What I didn't know was that Lilli had a particularly vicious and evil-tempered Scottish terrier touring with her. It was very fond of Lilli and totally allergic to everybody else. Arthur Barbosa had been to see me in Birmingham and was coming up with me to Liverpool to see his family. He had the most miserable journey sharing the back seat with the terrier, which snarled at him continually and went for him if he so much as moved. This, combined with Lilli's German accent, was quite enough to bring on one of those fits of the vapors for which Arthur was renowned. Usually they were caused by lack of drink, or claustrophobia, or boredom; in this instance he had all three to contend with, plus a nasty dog.

Lilli, I learned, was in England only because of Hitler. At

the time of her birth, her parents were living in Poznan, in a part of Poland which in 1921 became German. Her father, a surgeon who died quite young, moved the family to Berlin, I am not sure when. They were a very solid, middle-class, German Jewish family, and if it hadn't been for the Nazis, I imagine Lilli would have become a famous actress in Germany. She had been in a repertory theatre in Darmstadt when Hitler started his purge, and had left Germany in good time in the company of Dr. Rolf Gerard, a stage designer with whom, some years later, I became good friends. Eventually she got her mother and two sisters out as well.

None of this information relieved Arthur's vapors. On the contrary, he sank deeper and deeper into a trancelike state, aggravated no doubt by the impossibility of moving, lest he be savaged by the black beast at his side. When we reached Liverpool we deposited Lilli and the beast at her hotel, and I then drove a very rattled Arthur home, no doubt to down a considerable amount of his father's whisky.

I soon found Lilli to be a steadfast, reliable, stalwart person. She was not overburdened with our particular English sense of humor, but she had other sterling qualities. Our tours went their separate ways, but I was much taken by her honesty. She had told me of her struggles in getting out of Germany, and I had told her of my own difficulties, and a bond was formed. She lived with her family in Hampstead, and we saw a great deal of each other in London when our tours ended and I returned to my flat.

Meanwhile, when I was in Newcastle in December, Carol Reed came up to ask me to play in *Night Train to Munich,* costarring with Margaret Lockwood. In America, where it was called simply *Night Train,* this film was to run for fifteen weeks in New York during the war, and to lead eventually to my first Hollywood contract. We agreed to make it in the spring of 1940, which would coincide nicely with the end of the tour of *Design for Living.*

Carol Reed is another of those brilliant directors with a

Night Train to Munich

gift for relaxing actors. Carol may not be quite as easygoing a person as Victor Saville, but he gives the impression of relaxation, together with a sort of intensity lacking in Victor. He's careful, he's technical, he's a perfectionist, and he's marvelous with actors. In *Night Train to Munich* we had one scene with a lot of elderly actors. They were all German admirals, and I was a spy, dressed up as a German officer. Charlie France was playing the admiral in command of the German fleet, and though it wasn't a long scene he kept on forgetting his lines —he must then have been about seventy. I had very little to do, and only a few lines, and the old man was getting rather flustered, so Carol drew me to one side and said, "Rex, *you* forget *your* lines in this take. Before Charlie has his, you forget yours." So I fluffed away and apologized profusely; Carol asked me to try again, I did another take, and fluffed again. And by that time Charlie France had recovered his composure. The sight of someone else fluffing like that gave him huge confidence, and he sailed through the scene. The maneuver was typical of Carol's consideration for actors of every age and description.

The film finished in June, and by then with the evacuation of the British Expeditionary Force from Dunkirk the war was no longer phony, so Carol and I joined the Chelsea branch of the Home Guard. We made several abortive attempts to join something grander before resorting to this. We had been to the recruiting office of the Guards to make inquiries and were nearly enlisted as guardsmen, without so much as a by-your-leave, which was not quite our idea; and we had driven out to an airfield to see a Wing Commander friend of Carol's who, if we had not beaten a hasty retreat, would have set us there and then to guarding airfields as Air Force policemen. The Home Guard would have been a scream if it hadn't been so serious. It was a mixed bag of civilians and First World War veterans of uncertain age, totally unarmed. We were living in cloud-cuckoo-land, I suppose, but we expected to be invaded hourly, and we hoped we might be issued with arms, if not with uniforms, and make ourselves useful killing off at least a few Germans as they arrived.

The Chelsea Home Guard was commanded by a distinguished old gentleman called Sir Herbert Gough, who had joined the Sixteenth Lancers in 1889 and fought his way to the Khyber Pass with the Tirah Expedition of 1897. In the First World War he had been the first commander of the Fifth Army in France, knighted in 1916. Now, leading the Home Guard in Chelsea, the old general seemed untroubled by past glories and disappointments. Our field exercises consisted in the main of hurling imaginary grenades at him, as he appeared and disappeared around corners; and if the whole conception of the Home Guard now seems ridiculous, it was then, because of the gravity of the situation, very moving.

I had a platoon of veterans under my command, and for all the square-bashing in the Officers' Training Corps at Liverpool College, I knew very little about what I was doing; I could just about call them to attention. When one of the old boys asked me if I would like him to help in any way, I said, "I'd love you to."

"Don't love me to—tell me to," came the tart reply. I felt very squashed, and to save face ordered them in my best sergeant-major's voice to go and guard Chelsea Bridge.

About this time the government decided it was important to keep up the morale of the country in other ways too, and issued an edict that key actors should remain at their posts as actors and entertainers and be exempt from the services. This question was debated at a number of meetings in Drury Lane, where I remember hearing John Clements speak to the subject. I tried to make the point that the "key actors" the government had in mind should be named and clearly identified, but was told to pipe down, and, as I recall, John Clements went on talking.

In that summer of 1940, not long before the onset of the Battle of Britain, I was offered a part in the film of Bernard Shaw's *Major Barbara*. Gabriel Pascal was directing it, with

Wendy Hiller in the title role. Harold French was the dialogue director, and the now famous David Lean was the cutter.

Up till then I had stayed on in Sloane Street. Although Lilli was having troubles of her own as an enemy alien and was under curfew hours—she could not leave her Hampstead home after dark—we managed to see a lot of each other. But now, as the bombs began to fall, I was asked by the film producers to move out of London. I took a small cottage near the studios in Denham, and we decided that it would be safer for Lilli if she joined me there while I made the film.

Lilli was always open and straightforward, but even so the pressure for us to get married was now on. She came from a straitlaced family, and she wanted to be made an honest woman, as well as just being honest. Collette on the other hand was quite happy without a divorce and content to cruise along in her own way; she was getting money from me and enjoying her work in the Red Cross. But after a tug-of-war she agreed to sue for divorce, naming Lilli as corespondent.

All these issues had to be debated and settled while I was filming *Major Barbara,* which was a strange enough experience in itself without the added complication of domestic dramas. We had spotters on the roof of the studios who, when they sighted enemy aircraft, sounded off a Klaxon down below on the sound stage; all the boys came sliding down ropes from the platforms where the lights were, and we retreated into storage spaces underneath the concrete floor of the sound stage until the aircraft had moved out of our area, then went back and picked up the scene where we had left off. It was a fairly disjointed way of making a film.

At night I went back to my cottage in the woods while the Germans circled overhead dropping their loads on London. We were on the outside perimeter of their turn and not in the line of attack, except for the occasional accident or a German pilot feeling too nervous to face the barrage of anti-aircraft guns in central London.

Harold French had also had to move out of London, but

Riding with Lilli

his wife, Phyl, had a war job in town and stayed on in their
house. One morning when he came into my dressing room to
make his usual telephone call to see that all was well with her,
he could only get the unobtainable note. He went gray and
set off for London immediately. The unobtainable note could
have meant that *a* house in his street had been hit . . . but
it was Harold's house, and with Phyl dead amid the wreckage.

He went back to where he had been staying, in the country,
for a while, and then came to stay with me. I tried in every
way I could to help him through his grief, but in this situation
there is really nothing one can say, one can only be there. We
grew very close during that period and have remained so
ever since.

68

With George Bernard Shaw and Gabriel Pascal
on the set of *Major Barbara*

George Bernard Shaw came down to the studios one morning to record a foreword to the film. I was immensely impressed by his appearance. He wore a gray Norfolk jacket, gray knee breeches, long gray stockings, brogues, and a woolen tie. He was six foot two and very erect, with the most piercing blue eyes I had ever seen. His hair was quite white, and his beard also. With him came his famous secretary, Miss Patch, an old lady who appeared to me to be growing a small white moustache to match his.

All had been made ready for him, and he sat down at the desk he had asked should be provided and, though none of us knew what he was going to say or do, indicated that he was ready. The cameras were started. He sat bent over the desk, then looked up as though surprised to be thus discovered, and embarked on his speech.

It was directed at American audiences, and I can still recall one line: "You have sent us some of your old destroyers, and I am sending you film versions of some of my old plays." This was before the United States had come into the war, but it had already made some fifty destroyers available to us in return for the lease of some of our air bases.

The speech was a delight, and it went on and on until suddenly, as was evident from Gabriel Pascal's worried face, something went awry. Pascal started flapping about; G.B.S. was oblivious. Eventually Pascal crept up to the great man and touched him on the arm—G.B.S. looked around furiously, and Pascal confessed, "We've run out of film."

"Run out of what?" roared G.B.S., who was, I imagine, fairly ignorant of such technical necessities.

It was explained to him that he must stop, to allow the cameras to reload, and then go on. The delay threw him completely. He lost his train of thought, he fumbled and mumbled and dried up like any novice actor. I was fascinated to see this happen to a self-possessed man of such renowned intelligence. It took several reloads of the camera for him to finish what he wanted to say.

Afterward, Pascal asked him if he would read through the last scene between Major Barbara and Cusins and help us to interpret it. Wendy Hiller and I sat on either side of Shaw while he silently read through the long scene. There was a pause. Then he said, almost to himself, and with a strong Irish brogue, "Ah, what a terrible scene." It was exactly what we had thought. But there were no further words of wisdom forthcoming from the great man, I think because by then he was thoroughly exhausted.

Later on I was invited to lunch with him at Ayot St. Lawrence. But I had promised to take Noel out to lunch that day and could not let him down; most reluctantly I had to decline the invitation. G.B.S. was reported as saying, "He's a

fool—he can see his son any time, he may never see me again."
Shaw was then in his eighties—and I was a fool and I never did
see him again.

As many people will know, Gabriel Pascal had the film rights
to all of Shaw's plays and had paid for those rights the grand
sum of ten shillings, which was all he had in the world at the
time. The relationship between the two men was a heart-
warming example of two opposite types with complete trust
in each other. Shaw adored charlatans and indeed wrote about
a great many of them, Doolittle *père* in *Pygmalion* being a
prime example, and in return Pascal worshiped Shaw and
treasured his every line. Nothing could have persuaded Pascal
to debase Shaw's work, and Shaw knew it. Pascal is a book in
himself, a Hungarian like Korda, but very different. He was
a marvelous gypsy rogue, with incredible panache and no
guile, as open as a baby and as ruthless as a tiger. I adored
Gabriel, he really caught one's imagination.

We had some wonderful actors in the film, including some
notorious drunks. A watch was kept on the dressing rooms for
odd bottles of Scotch, but nothing was ever found—and yet
darling Robert Newton and Donald Calthrop seemed invariably to be carrying a heavy load. Eventually we discovered
that each of them had a hidey-hole on the set where he kept
a supply of nectar, and instead of retiring below during air
raids they sat chatting and imbibing, oblivious to danger,
until the rest of us came back to work. They were both marvelous actors, though Robert Newton for one could be a little
less good when sober. Donald Calthrop had an odd trick for
relaxing before a take: he would exhale all the breath from
his lungs and hang like a dead sparrow on his spindly legs until
the time came to speak. It always worried me that he never
appeared to inhale at all.

David Lean was known to us then as "the whispering cutter."
It was part of his job to give Pascal guidance even on the set,
but so that it should not be too obvious he insisted on whispering his advice into Gabriel's ear—which of course made it

far more obvious than if he had come on and shouted his head off.

When *Major Barbara* was finished, I accepted a part in the London production of S. N. Behrman's *No Time for Comedy*. Lilli and I planned to be married as soon as my divorce came through, and there was a part in the play for her too. It was to be presented by Binkie Beaumont and staged at the Haymarket, with Diana Wynyard as my leading lady. *No Time for Comedy* was about an author trying to write a serious play and getting out of his depth because his métier was writing comedies. It was a brilliantly constructed piece, with a seriousness of purpose under the veneer of sophistication.

It was through Sam Behrman that I met Peter Daubeny, who has run the World Theatre Season at the Aldwych, and who, though I have never worked for him, has been a staunch friend to me through thick and thin. After the war he went into theatre management, when he was still very young, and has since given to the theatre-going public innumerable productions which would never have been seen in England if it were not for his determination and his tirelessness. He has traveled immense distances every year to bring foreign companies to the Aldwych, and has had a great deal of ill health to contend with, but he never lets anything defeat him. I admire him enormously.

No Time for Comedy opened in Blackpool, and while we were on tour it was my job to know where all the shelters were. If an air-raid warning sounded, I stopped the play and went down to the footlights and explained, "Ladies and gentlemen, for those who want to leave the theatre . . ." and gave instruction as to how to reach the nearest shelters. For those who wanted to stay, I added, we would go on with the play. I gave them a few minutes to make up their minds, and since the curtain had not been lowered, I'd sit down on the stage and light a cigarette and wait to see what happened. Hardly

72

anybody did leave, but we soon discovered that after the interruption, the audience was no longer listening to the play. It was like having nobody there. When you stop to think of it, a theatre is rather like an eggshell—one bomb on the roof and you've had it. The people out front seemed to be frozen stiff, listening not to us but to the planes. So was I, for that matter, but I had to remember the lines and get on with it, and the exercise in concentration helped.

When we arrived in London it was hailing down bombs. We played the most extraordinary hours. We never did a night show—nobody came out at night—but there were morning performances and afternoon performances. Twice a week I was on fire-watch duty at the Haymarket, which became my second home; I had a bed in my dressing room and patrolled the building for incendiaries. There was a lot of bombing in that area, and one night the hotel at the back of the stage door was completely demolished. We never knew, when we came out in the morning to do a show, what would still be standing. A weird feeling, when you look back on it.

I was still resentful of the government's refusal to name "key actors" who were to be exempted from service, and especially now that we were in London I was plagued with guilt about not being in uniform. So eventually, without consulting anyone, I went in front of an RAF board.

They were a very distinguished lot of high-ranking officers, and the first thing they asked me was whether I realized I was exempt. I retorted that nobody had specified who were "key actors," that I had acted in the theatre for quite some time during the blitz and now wanted to make some other contribution, however small, to the war effort. They put their heads together and finally agreed that if this was how I felt, then probably I would not regret it.

On February 4, 1942, I was sent to Uxbridge, to the RAF depot, on a six-week Officers' Training Course. Back to the

73

old square-bashing and rifle drill of Liverpool College, only more so, and in bitterly cold weather. I had all my hair cut off, and I slept in a room with forty other men; the assorted noises that a group of men can make in the night are beyond belief. Unpleasant as it was, I have to admit that when I had finished the course I felt better than ever before in my life. I couldn't think what had happened to me, I felt so well.

At the end of the six weeks I was sent to the Photographic Reconnaissance Unit at Benson, an airfield just outside Oxford, as a Flying Control Officer. My commanding officer here turned out to be Hugh Wakefield, the comedian with whom I had driven through the New Forest to stay with the Duchess of Westminster, when I ended up axle-deep in a pond. But either he had not read my account of the incident in *Lilliput,* or he had the decency not to mention it.

Lilli at this time was having difficulties, particularly under the restrictions of her curfew. I'd been able to get out of the Uxbridge barracks a couple of times for meals at the cottage with her, but when I went to Benson I was not allowed to have her near the camp. Nor could I go to visit her, because she was working.

In the summer of 1942, however, my divorce came through, and while I was on leave Lilli and I were married. The wedding was a quiet affair, at Caxton Hall Registry Office in London. My best man, and boon companion at the prenuptial celebrations, was Arthur Barbosa, who was now a dashing officer in the Pay Corps, an outfit he had wisely lit upon as being the least likely to involve him in active combat and increase his vapors.

On my return to Benson I was reposted and sent to be trained as a Flying Control Liaison Officer. The course was held at Rudlow Manor—I could hardly believe my ears when I heard I was going back to Buster Tonge's old house. It was now Ten Group Operational Command. The lovely croquet lawn had become a motor-transport yard, and the drawing room where so many bottles of whisky had been quietly consumed was now the Air Marshal's office, while I was quartered in a Nissen hut, miles away from the house. An abrupt change in my fortunes.

I was what they called a Pilot Officer penguin, which meant that although a Pilot Officer I had no wings. It was one of the lowest positions in the Air Force, but it was the best I could do: because of the measles, all those years ago in Sheffield, I had vision in only one eye.

Flying Control Liaison was invented by Wing Commander "Death" Bulmore, so called because he used to take part in flying circuses before the war. Its basic objective was to try to save S.O.S. bombers returning from night raids over Germany, by getting them down into the nearest airfield, as soon as they reached the coast, or, if they came down in the sea, by sending Air-Sea Rescue to pick them up out of the water. The course was tough but interesting. We had many aids at our disposal to help the bombers, most of them on the secret list, and we learned all the intricacies of radar, then in its early days.

I passed the course exam and stayed on three or four months at Rudlow, until I was sent to the famous Eleven Group Headquarters, which was back at Uxbridge. This was the operational group for the whole of southern and eastern England, facing the enemy in France and Holland. The operations room, the most interesting place anywhere in the war, was down in the bowels of the earth and was called by all and sundry "The Hole." We went down some hundreds of feet in great iron elevators, and along endless passages, to reach the room, which was shaped like an elongated egg. The controllers of operations were on one side of the egg, behind glass, and the other side was covered with boards detailing the squadrons and their state of readiness. In the middle of the egg was an enormous table covered with a large-scale map of our sector, down from the Wash and around the Thames

Estuary, and along the south coast as far as Southampton, and also of the enemy area along the French and Belgian coast, up to the Dutch islands.

Around the table sat twenty or thirty WAAF's with earphones on, plotting aircraft—ours and the enemy's; we could tell at a glance who was up on the enemy side and who on ours. The girls had counters representing different numbers of aircraft—200 plus, or 50 plus, or even just 1—and they moved them with long poles, such as croupiers use, as the aircraft were picked up by radar or by the Observer Corps dotted about the country. It was an astonishing sight. The Americans later used the system as a model, and we always had high-ranking American officers coming in as observers.

I worked in one of the glass cages on the perimeter of the room and found my job fascinating. As well as showing the number of aircraft up in the air, the counters on the table also detailed the S.O.S. aircraft, and these were my baby. I might have as many as twenty S.O.S. aircraft on the board at one time, and they all had to be contacted and directed to airports where they could land; or, if the aircraft was over the Channel, I would have the naval authorities put up beacons on the headlands, at Portland Bill and Beachy Head, and alert Air-Sea Rescue. I had at least five telephones, each for its particular purpose.

Always my activities reached their peak around dawn, when our bombers were coming back, and the night watches were exhausting. I had a WAAF working with me who logged what I was doing so that I could answer all inquiries the next day. Air staff were always quick to ask what steps had been taken to save aircraft in distress, and if you got all the S.O.S. aircraft of the night down safely you really did feel you had done something to help.

Along with tours of duty in the operations room, we also kept watches around the fighter airfields, to see at first hand how our first aid to aircraft was working. One night when I was down at Manston, a Fighter Command field in the south-east corner of England, a bomber in our area started sending distress signals, radioing two dead and not much aircraft left. The Germans used to send their bombers back with ours sometimes, to catch just such aircraft as this, so we knew we might well have an enemy bomber in the circuit too. We rang the station commander for permission to put all the lights on anyway, in the hope of getting our aircraft in. We put the cones up and waited in the control tower to get blown to bits, but as we concentrated on bringing in our plane, with its crew of dead and injured men, we gradually forgot about the Germans.

Then, instead of bombs, we saw in the lights a host of little objects floating down, like large jam jars with small propellers whirring away on top of them. These were something new: antipersonnel bombs. If you walked too near one it would at the very least take a leg off. They settled in the grass all around us, while we concentrated on our plane, finally got it down, and ran out to it to bring out the crew —heedless of jam jars.

The aircraft was in an appalling mess, bringing me suddenly hard up against the horrors of war. After we had got everyone out (and sent the boys who were still alive off to Intelligence), we had a long, long walk back to the mess in the dark, not knowing from one minute to the next when we were going to meet up with a jam jar. I retired to bed badly shaken, while the bomber boys, those who were alive and able to continue, were taken off by car after their session with Intelligence. They were sent back to Liverpool Street Station, where they were put on special trains that whisked them down to their bomber bases in East Anglia and Cambridgeshire, so that they should be in time for the briefing for the next night's work. They were incredible—as they drove off into the night they were already cracking jokes.

While I was at Uxbridge, Lilli lived in the house I had rented in Denham near the film studios, where I could go when I was on leave. Deborah Kerr and Harold French were

With Harold French

visiting us there one day when I heard an airplane circling around, quite near us, under a very low ceiling. I thought it might be trying to get into one of the local airfields, such as Northolt. I was standing at the window and suddenly saw, coming out of the overcast and seemingly no more than fifty feet above the trees, a German aircraft. As I watched—it was like one frame of a film—a bomb came off the rack. I had just time to shout a warning; the next thing I knew I was at the other end of the room and smoke was everywhere. Luckily it had been raining heavily and the ground was soft: the bomb had gone in deep before exploding. Lilli had a cut wrist, but Deborah and Harold weren't hurt; I had a cut on the forehead, and about a week later found my chest and shoulders bruised black and blue by the blast. The top of the house had been totally demolished. If the bomb had exploded on hard ground, it would have killed the four of us.

While I was still in the Air Force our son was born, and we christened him Carey Alfred. He arrived during one of the worst raids of the war, and though the London Clinic was not hit I got Lilli and the baby out of London at the first available opportunity.

I remained at Eleven Group for two years, until Air Force Command posted me back to my entertainment duties: they now had an adequate supply of Flying Control Liaison Officers trained. I was honorably discharged and left the Air Force to make the film of Noël Coward's *Blithe Spirit*.

The director of *Blithe Spirit* was none other than the "whispering cutter," David Lean. By now he has a great many films to his credit, but then he was only just coming over from film editing to directing. He was given much encouragement by Noël Coward, who saw his potential; even though Noël was disappointed with *Blithe Spirit,* he went on to give Lean *Brief Encounter,* which set him on the road to success.

I was rusty after all those years away from the set, and to start with was all fingers and thumbs. David Lean was ill at ease with comedy and his tension communicated itself to me. I remember one occasion when I had struggled through a scene in rehearsal, and Lean turned to Ronald Neame, his cameraman, and said, "I don't think that's very funny, do you?" Neame echoed, "I don't think it's very funny, no." They could hardly have thought of a better way to hamstring an actor. In those days, I suspect, Lean seemed to feel that actors were an irksome necessity who had to be tolerated until such time as he could get his hands on the celluloid and indulge his real passion, which was for editing.

Kay Hammond was playing Elvira, the ghost wife. It was the first time we had been together since *French Without Tears,* and it was lovely to be acting with her again. But the making of this film was a difficult experience for all concerned, and there was little fun or relaxation to be had from it.

Lilli and I bought a small house on the Denham golf course and lived there for some time while I made two further films. *I Live in Grosvenor Square* I did with Anna Neagle—it was not a film of great consequence, but after the years on Air Force pay the coffers needed refilling. *The Rake's Progress* on

ABOVE *Blithe Spirit* with Constance Cummings and Kay Hammond
(Photos - Rank)
BELOW With Lilli in *The Rake's Progress*

the other hand has become a classic of its kind. It was written and directed by Sidney Gilliat, a lovely man with a heart of gold and a great sense of humor. *Rake's Progress* was in effect a portrait of a kind of young man who was often to be met with in those days. As he lies dying in a disused farmhouse, during the war, he reviews his life in flashback. Sidney's style, debonair and touching, suited me down to the ground. I loved the part, and found Sidney a meticulous but enormously kind and understanding director. (In America the title of the film was changed to *Notorious Gentleman*—for fear, the distributors said, that *The Rake's Progress* be taken for a gardening adventure.)

The war ended while I was making these films, and the producer Basil Dean asked me if I would go out and entertain the troops still stationed in Europe. So I donned a strange khaki outfit, with the initials ENSA on my sleeve, and took old *French Without Tears* around Holland, Belgium, France, and Germany. Roland Culver came too, playing his original part, and Anna Neagle took over Kay Hammond's former role.

Paris was under military control, but great gaiety went on nonetheless. We played the Marigny Theatre in the Champs-Elysées, while the Old Vic company, with Olivier and Richardson, played the Comédie Française. After the performances we went around the town on foot and had a lot of fun. It was in Paris that Roland Culver landed a Hollywood contract and left for California. I was to see him again, out there, very shortly, but at the time I had no inkling of it. The rest of the tour, in the other countries, was very grim. But the troops enjoyed the show, and we were packed every night with enthusiastic audiences.

On my return to London I joined Lilli at the Savoy Hotel and found urgent messages awaiting me from one Taft Schreiber, an emissary from Hollywood's MCA Agency. He had been trying to trace me, he complained, all over Europe; he had to meet me, he said, at once.

He brought with him a very fat contract from Twentieth

Century–Fox, which according to Schreiber they were offering me largely on the strength of *Night Train*. They wanted seven years with options. A lot of money was involved, and the first film was named: it was *Anna and the King of Siam*. I was excited, but being by nature cautious asked to read the script first; I liked it so agreed to go.

I had certain misgivings about what I was taking on, but still we packed up and sold our house to John and Mary Mills. We left Denham on a brilliant September morning, and looking at the glistening countryside I wondered what the hell was going to happen to me. I had a presentiment that I had started down a very long road to somewhere—God alone knew where.

CHAPTER FIVE

Lotus Land

Entering the lotus land of Southern California at that time, 1945, was bound to be a shock, considering what it was like at home—the war, rationing, the extraordinary feeling of all pulling together. Of course, one of my fears was that I might like it—that I might be seduced by its ease and richness and laziness, and lose my drive. Actors like Leslie Howard had come back from Hollywood full of cautionary tales. But I needn't have worried.

We crossed the Atlantic in one of the *Queens* which was still ferrying American soldiers home; we were about the only civilians on board. The dining rooms were packed throughout the day with men eating in shifts, and the decks covered with sleepy soldiers lying mattress to mattress. I will never forget the reception as the ship steamed up the Hudson. Boats came out with bands, girls sang and danced, and there were parties for the boys on the dock. It was an enormously colorful and exciting moment, even though I had no part in it. Equally vividly, I remember the three nights and two days in the train—we traveled on the Super Chief through miles and miles of groves, grapefruit and orange and other things I'd never seen before—and the arrival at Pasadena. As on the day I'd left Denham, it was a beautiful morning, but the light was totally different from that which I had left, a harder light altogether.

We were met by a most enthusiastic agent who, from the moment I alighted from the train, kept on saying, "Gee, you're just like the King of Siam! Gee, you look so much like the King of Siam!" I thought, Well, I wonder. Not quite sure I like that. I can't really look like the King of Siam. However, I thought he simply meant well—until I found that this was the reaction of all and sundry on my arrival. They all gave me the impression that I looked like a very small Oriental king of the 1870s. This really worried me.

On my first visit to the Fox studios, when I went to meet John Cromwell, the director, I was naturally nervous. I knew I was going to have to lean on him; I had envisaged him, when I was reading the script in the Savoy Hotel in London, as one of those brilliant people who would be able to tell me how to approach the part. He turned out to be a very tall New Englander with a nose like a corkscrew, who seemed kindly but extremely aloof. At least two months passed before the production began, during which time, if we did come across each other, he withdrew, either physically or mentally; I was never able to sit down with him and discuss my fears and worries about playing an Oriental, and he never told me what he thought about the character.

The producer was Louis Lighton, a highly intelligent man who had difficulty in articulating his thoughts. He talked in riddles, so abstruse that I used to sit in his office and try in vain to make out their meaning. Poor man, he was losing his sight very rapidly, so perhaps he could be excused for thinking I looked like the King of Siam. Darryl Zanuck ran the studio, but he was far too busy to talk to actors about their roles. I caught sight of him just once or twice, walking from his office to the cafeteria, holding a riding crop and dressed for polo.

This lackadaisical attitude was not at all what I'd expected, and I began feeling pretty desperate. Everything was so slow;

I wasn't geared to relaxing around pools and drinking all day. I'd been used all my life to working hard, and now suddenly I was in a hot bath, growing weaker and weaker. The sets were only just being constructed, so there was no hope of beginning for weeks, and in the meantime there was nobody I could talk to constructively about how I was to tackle this frightfully difficult role, for which I was far too young and two feet too tall.

We took a suite of rooms at the Beverly Hills Hotel, but shortly afterward rented a house from Clifton Webb, the Broadway entertainer, dancer, and musical-comedy man, who was then in Hollywood. The house was in Bel Air, which is a big, rather elaborate residential area, where the houses are all much of a muchness, but quite pretty, with gardens and pools. Ours was high up in the hills, and it had a tiny garden where I used to pace, day after day, like a caged animal, with the script in my hands, trying to work out what the devil I was going to do. I could see the studios away in the distance—in those days there was no smog, you could see right across to the Fox studios—and I got more and more frightened of the unknown. At Denham I had been able to discuss problems with people like Victor Saville, or even with Korda, who was always accessible, and although a businessman was undoubtedly an artist too. If you had a problem on your mind, such as this, you could go to Korda, and he would sit down and give you marvelous advice. But here I was left high and dry.

During this waiting period, however, we began to make friends, mostly within the English colony. We met Ronald Colman and Benita, his wife, and Tyrone Power and his wife, Annabella, and even before I had made that first picture we started going out and about—there was nothing else for us to do. Saturday night out was a must, and we would go from one house to another, meeting the same people all the time, and then asking people back to our little house. I met a lot of musicians too, and on one occasion Benny Goodman came to our house, which gave me a great thrill. We became friendly

with Irene Selznick, David Selznick's first wife, and she introduced us to her father, Louis B. Mayer; through Ronnie Colman we met Sam Goldwyn and his wife, Frances, who used to give marvelous parties.

I used to feel, at those parties, like a film fan who had wandered in off the street. While I was making my movies in England, I'd spent a great many Sunday evenings at the Empire, Leicester Square, and seen the great movie stars—Gable and Cooper, Cary Grant, James Stewart, Spencer Tracy. When faced with them now, suddenly finding them collected together in one room, I just stood and stared at them. I was like a schoolboy. They didn't stare at me—they didn't know me from a hole in the ground. I was just a new English actor

*Anna
and the King of Siam*
(20th Century–Fox)

who'd come out on a contract to Fox, while they were giants, standing there chatting away. It took me quite a long time to be able to relax enough to speak at all, but I had to stick with them, because there was an extraordinary convention, in these long California drawing rooms, whereby all the men went to talk at one end of the room and all the women gathered at the other end.

The conversation between those great male stars I found most strange, totally different from what I was used to. The actors I had known in London before going into the Air Force were forever hurrying from one place to another, rehearsing, running for work, snatching a meal in a café. They were working actors, talking about their jobs, their profession, and

87

I could still remember Tyrone Guthrie giving me a terrible dressing down for having a car; it was a sign, he said, that I wasn't serious. I should be walking or, better still, running to work, not giving in to the fleshpots with a fifteen-pound car. That was the kind of attitude I was accustomed to finding in actors, but these Hollywood stars talked like sportsmen, about their last fishing trip up the Rogue River, their last hunting trip to Colorado, how their guns were functioning, their vacations to the Far East or to Europe. They were, by and large, much more like very rich, very well-informed ranchers. They were, I found, very much more handsome even than on the screen. They never talked about acting, quite rightly, because they didn't act. They were themselves. He *was* Gary Cooper, he *was* Clark Gable, he *was* James Stewart—they didn't have to act, they were it.

The girls at the other end of the room were another story. They were quite pretty, flirtatious, mostly having come up the hard way. They knew their way around, sometimes better than the ranchers, I thought.

I felt pretty insignificant in that society. I wished I looked more like a rancher. I thought I should have much more hair, look much tougher, and speak more slowly, with a drawl, and even sit sometimes for hours, just staring.

Sometime later I found myself sharing a bungalow at the Monterey Hotel with Gable. We were on a golfing weekend with David Niven and Nigel Bruce but spent the first day fishing, and Gable hadn't spoken to me at all. He'd gone out in a canoe, and just sat; he'd had a bottle of beer for lunch, he hadn't caught any fish, and he'd gone on sitting, literally, making no effort to talk to me. He didn't know who I was, or if he did, he was lost in his own thoughts. A lot of these men had been born in hill country, where people do sit and stare and say nothing—this was sometimes a part of their success. Think of Gary Cooper's "Yup," which became so famous. Cooper would take a script and cut the speeches down to almost nothing, and he was a marvelous screen actor precisely because he looked terrific and said little. He just did it with his face and with his eyes, very wise. It was a lesson I was beginning to learn.

Anyway, all of a sudden, Gable started to grumble. I always think all actors should grumble. Gable had a few Scotches and began to unburden himself, and now he became something much more than a rancher. I felt suddenly I was in the presence of an actor. He grumbled, obviously about Metro-Goldwyn-Mayer, and the parts they'd been giving him lately, and how unhappy he'd been with them, how they'd worn him down and mistreated him—all the usual actor's grumbles. I had nothing to contribute, of course, I'd only known him on the silver screen, but I sat there enjoying his royal discontent. I just thought he was what they called him, the King, I accepted him as the King, and he was a magnificent man. It was, to me, a rather marvelous moment.

When we started to shoot *Anna and the King of Siam* I had no one like Gable to turn to for advice. I'd done wardrobe tests, I'd done makeup tests—I had quite an elaborate makeup and had to have a plaster cast made of my head, and small rubber attachments so that my eyes, on the inside, would look Oriental and not Occidental. It didn't greatly change my appearance, but it helped. Costume and makeup were, I think, the most efficient of the departments I struck before we started filming.

Still without help I went to work, and having worked on the part for so long on my own, with no real contact with John Cromwell, I had to take my own course. This only widened the gap between us, because Cromwell saw that I wasn't waiting for him. I'd play each scene as I'd prepared it, to the best of my ability, always suspecting that I could never really get inside the mind of the King of Siam, and John Cromwell, from the beginning, just left it, never trying to make suggestions or improvements. It was, I think, the last film that he made in Hollywood, and I suspect, although I haven't seen him since those days, that he was as disillusioned with Hollywood as anybody around and had given up, packed it in.

With Irene Dunne he seemed to have a better working relationship than he had with me. She was an excellent actress, much more used to the Hollywood scene than I was. She too went her own way, and tactfully used the director, as I later learned to do myself, to her own advantage; she listened to what he had to give, and discarded it or used it, as she wished.

The filming went on for, I think, five months. Louis Lighton helped as much as possible and, about three-quarters of the way through the filming (I'm sure without Zanuck's knowledge), ran the printed dailies for me and pointed out some of the things I could have done better, making suggestions for the latter stages of the filming which were very useful to me.

I met only one real producer-artist in Hollywood in my first stay there, and that was David Selznick. He was a genius and a great film maker who loved actors and understood them. He had none of the problems of the old regime out there, the men who'd gone out to Hollywood from the nickelodeon days in New York, when they started filming in little movie huts, literally in cupboards. The moguls were rigid, but David Selznick was young and vigorous and had a wild enthusiasm for the moving-picture industry. Though I didn't meet him many times during that first visit, I did have a couple of talks with him about *Anna and the King of Siam,* and he was the only person to sit down with me and ask the central question: Why had I wanted to do it, why had I wanted to play the role of an Oriental King? He didn't say I looked like the King of Siam; he asked why—and I found this very reassuring. I saw as much of him as I could, but he was enormously busy. After making *Gone with the Wind,* he had gone on to tackle a lot of other very big subjects. I felt then, as now, that he was a giant in the film world. Happily I got to know him well in later years before his tragic death.

When *Anna and the King of Siam* was finished, there came

a disastrous period of seven months when Fox didn't produce a single thing that I wanted to do. I turned down one script, *13 rue Madeleine,* which they then gave to James Cagney. If James Cagney could play it, I certainly couldn't. It was a spy thriller in which the hero was a tough little American, or a tough big American—it doesn't matter which, he certainly wasn't me. I wanted to work, I didn't want to sit, but I didn't want to do what I didn't want to do.

They could have suspended me—I hadn't read the small print in my contract carefully enough to realize that contractually they could give me anything and, if I turned it down, say, "Right, off salary." Alternatively, they were entitled to lease me out to other studios. They did neither, and in this respect Fox was very good to me. But it was no consolation for the fact that they were confused by me and didn't know how to cast me. I didn't fit into the American scene of comedy; Cary Grant had cornered that market, and they couldn't see me in comedy at all. They regarded me as a peculiar-looking chap who, as the ex-King of Siam, was best qualified to be what they called a character man. But this of course was exactly the sort of part that I was not able to render in American terms, or in any other terms come to that.

Consequently I grew more and more fed up, waiting for work that did not materialize and meanwhile being paid large weekly checks. The terms of my contract gave me four thousand dollars a week for forty-six out of fifty-two weeks in the year, which was a very high wage in the Forties, and I soon found that the whole thing went to my head. The lavish living, the size of the steaks, the flowers, the alcoholic content of the whisky, the beauty of the women: it was all too much for me. There was nothing to do but go to parties, play golf, and go to the beach. This was ruinous for me. I was haunted by the fear that I was going to sink into this awful swamp and come to like it. I could see people around me literally decaying in front of my eyes—people who'd been out there longer than I had, who had lost the desire to work, or do anything

With Gene Tierney in *The Ghost and Mrs. Muir* (20th Century–Fox)

much; who lived out their lives, comfortable, luxurious, and lazy. And now I too did nothing. We went from party to party. We went to Palm Springs and back again. We met more and more people, more or less the same people. Except for the Saturday nights, it was a lonely existence too, and I think those months of not working go to explain in part why, while I was out there, my behavior was not all that could be desired. I was impatient and desperate and saying "Yup" too often to every-thing, except work. I started to compensate for not being able to stare into the middle distance by staring a little too closely—and not just at the steaks.

At last, after seven months of riotous and edgy living, a film came up that I did like, called *The Ghost and Mrs. Muir,* which I played with Gene Tierney. I'd met Gene, with her husband, Oleg Cassini, a dress designer of considerable note, at some of those endless soirees, and thought her very nice and quite out of the ordinary. The film was directed by Joe Man-kiewicz, with whom I was later to make three other films. It was rather a sweet story, about a young widow who rented a house on the cliffs, and the ghost of a dashing sea captain who haunted the house. The widow was inclined to believe the ghost was real, and there grew up between them a strange romantic relationship. The film was a great success and was eventually turned into a television series.

At this time Lilli decided to take up her career again and started to work like a beaver—extremely successfully too. She made *Cloak and Dagger* with Gary Cooper, *My Girl Tisa* with Sam Wanamaker, *Body and Soul* with John Garfield, *No Minor Vices* with Dana Andrews. After our first three or four months in Hollywood Lilli was very busy. I think she too felt that to do nothing in California was pretty dangerous.

Lilli had a greater tolerance for the Hollywood scene than I did. She had her work well organized, she was not tempera-mental. She never took a drink—except on one occasion, when she teamed up with Collette. Noel, who was then at prepara-

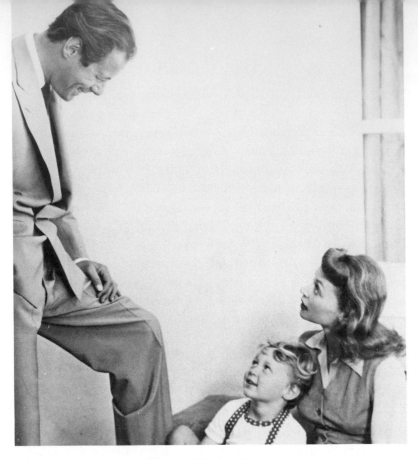

With Lilli and Carey

tory school at Sunningdale, came out to stay with us during one holiday—he arrived with the usual English look, bright blue and very skinny, and I think the air and sun did him good—and Collette traveled over with him. She stayed for some time at a hotel, but found it rather lonely, to my surprise, and eventually we invited her to stay with us in Bel Air. One evening when I was out working on a recording, she and Lilli also went out to have dinner together. I came back to the house at half past twelve and saw the garage door more or less bashed in two and wrapped around the front of the car. Upstairs I found Lilli absolutely passed out, stone cold on the bed, and in the other room, Collette, sleeping the sleep of the just. I woke her up and inquired what the hell she thought she was doing, getting Lilli smashed, and the car. Collette was apologetic and got up to see to things, while

I retreated in high dudgeon to the other end of the house.

With *The Ghost and Mrs. Muir* I'd slightly climbed out of the doldrums, and I managed to see Zanuck and ask him if he would buy the rights to make a film of John Galsworthy's *Escape*. Gerald du Maurier had made a film of it many years earlier, a silent film, with Basil Dean directing, and I knew the subject and thought it was something that I wanted to do. Meantime I started working on a film called *The Foxes of Harrow,* with Maureen O'Hara. I liked the script, and thought that at last I was getting into my stride, because this was a good part. A Mississippi River gambler wasn't perhaps my total image of myself, but at least I could fit into the part, particularly since they made him an Irishman, *and* with a Ronald Colman moustache.

In those days the Colman moustache was the accolade. It had been put on Laurence Olivier for *Rebecca,* and on David Niven, who still has it, on Errol Flynn and Douglas Fairbanks, Jr., in fact on almost any actor who was not a character man. It seemed I'd now made the big time, with my Colman moustache. While we were making the film, though, little notes used to come down from Zanuck to the producer: "It seems that Harrison's moustache is getting bigger. Please watch this." Of course if it had got too big I might have been demoted to character man again.

The Foxes of Harrow was directed by an old-timer, John M. Stahl, who knew his films well. In contrast to my first experience with John Cromwell, I found with Stahl and Mankiewicz, and later with Preston Sturges, that I got a lot of help, and I will always be grateful to them for what I learned.

I noticed that Hollywood technicians were undoubtedly ahead of the technicians we had had at the Denham studios. In England film making was still a growing industry, with lads doing jobs from which they expected to be quickly promoted, whereas Hollywood technicians were more highly paid and therefore remained in their positions. Among the technicians, the man who lights the set ranks higher than the camera operator who concentrates on keeping the actors in frame as they get up and down and move about. In America a camera operator would be a man of any age up to sixty; he wouldn't have moved up to a lighting man, because that was a slightly different job, and since he'd been in the one job for perhaps thirty years, he had vast experience and was totally expert. This applied all through the departments; even the carpenters —the "chippies"—were men of many years' experience. In British studios, where they were training the young men and everyone was climbing on everyone else's back, there was a certain inadequacy in the minor jobs. Boom operators got mike shadows into the shots, and camera operators were unable to pan the camera up quickly enough if you made a swift movement getting up from a chair. They'd say, "Will you please move a little slower? We can't get it"—a plea unheard of in Hollywood.

Though I was working again, and finding on the set people I got on with and whose professional competence I respected, I still felt deeply at odds with the Hollywood system. I had been an independent person ever since I'd left home, and I wanted to remain so. But I could see that actors of my standing, although well paid, were rather small fry in the Hollywood scheme of things, and I hadn't been prepared for the kowtowing that went on, even by the great, to the all-powerful newspapers and gossip columnists.

At Gary Cooper's house one night there was a big party at which, to my amazement, both the leading columnists, Louella Parsons and Hedda Hopper, were present. I was at a table which included Hopper and Gene Tierney, who had been temporarily estranged from her husband, Oleg Cassini. This was great meat for the columnists—at the slightest sign of anyone breaking up there were huge hurrahs and headlines. Now suddenly Hopper turned on Gene and said, "Why didn't you tell me you were pregnant? It's disgusting!" Disgusting, because Hopper hadn't been informed. Poor Gene, who had dared to be estranged from her husband and then reconciled without telephoning the columnists, was reduced to tears.

96

With Maureen O'Har
in *The Foxes of Harro*
(20th Century-Fox

There were all too few stars who didn't follow the established lines; I think probably 70 percent of them went right down the sucking-up line. Joe Cotten was the only person, apart from myself, who had a good go at them. His was a more physical and funnier go than mine. Louella Parsons was sitting in the Beverly Hills Hotel in a wicker chair, talking to someone, and Joe was passing by and gave her a great boot. She was well padded but I think she must have got the message all right.

There were of course some wonderful characters among the writers and actors who saved the place and who felt the same as I did. But many of them had come, like me, from a different background—Europe or England. Ronald Colman, for instance, gave a lot of dinner parties, but you certainly wouldn't see any columnists in his house. Ronnie was very independent and conservative where privacy was concerned. When David Niven's wife died and David used to go up to the Colmans' house and spend the days there, Sam Goldwyn—who'd produced all Colman's early films, and then later Niven's films— was admitted to the house for the first time in perhaps twenty years.

The columnists had started out trying to goad me, within the first four weeks of my arrival, by saying I loved the place so much that I was going to take out American citizenship papers. This was a lead, of course, intended to provoke a hot denial. They knew I would not have wanted such a story to get back to England. But no hot denial came forth. I'd sensed their game, and said very politely that if I'd had no other country of allegiance, I'd have been very happy to become an American citizen; as it was I was firmly rooted in my own country and saw no reason to change.

I was invited to appear in a comedy skit on the Eve Arden radio show, which included a comment on garden parties at Buckingham Palace. I declined the invitation when they assigned me a quip about King George VI being the English

Carole Landis (Keystone)

Atwater Kent—a millionaire whose Hollywood parties had been likened to "Coney Island with caviar." The columnists went to town on my refusal, and I was quoted as saying that the line "wounded my sensibilities."

About halfway through my stay in Hollywood, when I was working on *The Foxes of Harrow*, I met a girl who I thought, from talking with her a little, rather shared my views on Hollywood. She was ostracized and shunned by the people I used to meet in those California drawing rooms, shunned for the strange reason that she was, I think, ahead of her time.

Carole Landis was what might now be called a liberated woman, and she was frowned upon because of it. She was of Polish extraction, the daughter of immigrants who spoke very little English, and she came from Wisconsin. She had been married at the age of fifteen. Carole had had a marvelous war. She had gone around, with the zest which was typical of her, entertaining the troops, in all sorts of areas and under all sorts of hardship; she was very lovely to look at, and she could sing and entertain. She wrote a book about her experiences in Europe and North Africa called *Four Jills in a Jeep,* which was later made into a film. When I met her she was married to but estranged from Horace Schmidlapp, a New York businessman.

We met first on a weekend in Palm Springs, which was then little more than an oasis in the desert. I was sitting in the bar of the Racquet Club with Charlie Farrell and Lucille Ball, when Carole came in with a group of people. We were introduced and started talking. Carole was a warm, attractive girl, and soon we were swapping funny stories and limericks, sitting up late in the electric desert air.

Carole had a style that was, I think, imposed upon her by her war experience. She wore casual clothes, she was very good at meeting people, very good, obviously, with men, offhand and jolly. She was, when I met her, not very happy. She was quite ambitious and wanted to make films, but for reasons which I never got to the bottom of, she couldn't get into any studio. I don't say she was a talented actress, but she was a beautiful girl and full of life, and could certainly have fitted into many parts. But those were the days of the drawing rooms, the ranchers, and the ladies, so called, and nobody thought Carole was a lady. Well, what is a lady? While Carole was entertaining the troops during the war, she was famous for her warmth, her courage, and her unbelievable energy. Three years later she was looked on with mistrust.

I thought she was rather a marvelous person, and I liked her very much: I liked her freedom, I liked the way she talked, the way she looked. She was quite a girl, and we got on terribly well. For me, of course, it was also a great relief to meet another rebel, with similar and yet different views on the establishment and institutions of Hollywood in 1947. We began to see each other a lot, so much so that I found the drawing rooms receding from my life, and that I would rather go and play tennis with

Carole, or swim, or take a picnic to the beach. It became harder and harder not to meet, and we both knew something rather alarming had happened to us.

Finally my work on *The Foxes of Harrow* came to an end, and my next assignment was to work in England on Galsworthy's *Escape,* which the studio had kindly been persuaded to buy. It was the story of an escaped convict, wrongfully accused of murder, and was made partly on Dartmoor and partly in the studios in London. I remember one scene in particular, where the convict is on a river, fishing for his dinner, and falls into conversation with another fisherman who turns out to be a judge. In the play, there's a fine, long, philosophical scene between the judge and the convict, about justice and the law. Zanuck cut it out because he thought it was too slow, but I think this cut took away from the film much of its force.

As luck would have it, Carole had previously been engaged for a film in London. While I was running about escaping from Dartmoor prison, struggling through fog and over moor and being chased by prison dogs, she was working in London, but we managed to meet, almost every weekend, in Plymouth.

I finished *Escape* before Carole's engagement was over and returned to Hollywood to start on another film for Fox. I found Lilli busy filming, while Carey, who was still little, was learning to swim underwater in the pool of the house we had just bought in Mandeville Canyon—a beautiful house, with stables and a big garden, the first house that I really liked in California. One of Carey's instructresses was Esther Williams, clad in a gold swimming costume.

The new film was called *Unfaithfully Yours,* and it was written, directed, and produced by that rare genius Preston Sturges. It was about a celebrated conductor who believes that his young wife, played by Linda Darnell, was unfaithful to him with his male secretary while he was away on a concert tour. While he is conducting three—very different—pieces of music, he plays out fantasies in his mind, of killing her, or of forgiving her, or of shooting himself in a game of Russian

101

Another variation on the Ronald Colman moustache—the ultimate accolade at Twentieth Century–Fox in the 1940's; with Linda Darnell in *Unfaithfully Yours* (20th Century–Fox)

roulette with the male secretary. The ending, as in most of Sturges's films, is both happy and comic.

Preston was a man I loved, and he had an interesting background. His mother had left his father, who was a Chicago meat-packer, when Preston was about five years old. She carried him off with her to Europe, where they traveled from one capital city to another. His mother had apparently made friends with the dancer Isadora Duncan, who was later strangled to death when her scarf became entangled in a car wheel. Preston had moved in sophisticated company, from one "uncle" to another, in Istanbul, Budapest, Vienna, and all points west. This rubbed off; he viewed life with considerable humor, and yet he was a hard taskmaster, and his film dialogue was elaborate and literary. The title *Unfaithfully Yours* was obviously an echo of the title of his first play, *Strictly Dishonorable,* with which he had had a great success as a young man back in the 1930s. It's interesting how a writer's style and personal history nearly always follow him to the grave—Preston's mother it was who made those two titles, if nothing else except some lovers.

While Carole was still in England, we spoke regularly by transatlantic telephone, and I wrote her a good many letters. At last she returned and took a little house in Pacific Palisades, not more than ten minutes away from our house in Mandeville Canyon. Preston Sturges kept me busy going over my lines with a script girl and working with an orchestra conductor to acquire some semblance of authenticity. I had no time even to think, but I went on seeing Carole as often as I could.

My absence from the drawing rooms caused a certain amount of comment, and at some point Lilli decided it would be better if she left Hollywood. She wasn't making a film at the time, so she went to stay with friends in New York, leaving Carey behind in the house with his nurse. Carole and I continued to meet, especially at weekends and in the evenings; when my film was finished, we were free to spend our days together on the beach and in her pool. Our feeling for each other showed no sign of abating. From time to time Carole seemed to withdraw from what was going on around her, as though temporarily she had gone elsewhere, except in the physical sense; but in a few minutes she would be herself again, and I attached little significance to these times.

Just then I had a chance to do a play on Broadway, which thrilled me very much, for greatly as I had enjoyed working with Sturges, I was still restless for the theatre. When Leland Hayward offered me the part of Henry VIII in Maxwell Anderson's *Anne of the Thousand Days,* I saw it as a marvelous change of pace and a chance to get away from the lush life of Hollywood. Maxwell Anderson, who had written such plays as *High Tor, Winterset, Mary of Scotland,* and *Elizabeth the Queen,* had a lyric style and a great love of the Tudor period. I read this play and loved it, and as I always like to have friends' opinions on plays that interest me, I told Carole of the offer and asked her to read the script and let me know what she thought of it.

On the eve of July 4, the night before Leland was to take me down to Malibu Beach to meet Maxwell Anderson, I went up to Carole's for supper. Carole said she thought it a fascinating play and a marvelous part. She seemed a little down, but I was so high myself on the idea of getting back into the theatre that I'm afraid I didn't notice the extent of her downness. I left quite early to go over to see Roland Culver, my old friend from the days of *French Without Tears,* who was working out there for Paramount. I had given him a copy of the play too and was anxious to know what he thought about it before I met the author. Roland and I had a long chat, and I shouldn't think I left there much before one o'clock. I went home and called Carole to say good night, and at the back of my mind I thought, Well, she sounds a little strange—but I made nothing very much of it.

Leland picked me up in the morning to go and discuss the play with Anderson. We had a very good meeting in Malibu and a picnic lunch on the beach. Maxwell Anderson was a

strange big bear of a man with a marvelous mottled face, lots
of children, and a very nice wife called Mab. He gave one
an enormous feeling of goodwill, sweetness, and intelligence.
It was clear that he wanted me to play Henry VIII, so an ar-
rangement was made, and I agreed to make every effort to get
a release from my contract with the studio for the run of the
play.

Leland and I drove back, arranging to meet as soon as possible with Darryl Zanuck, to see if he would release me from
my contract. When I got home I called Carole to tell her that
I was back. The maid answered, and said she'd knocked on
Miss Landis's bedroom door a couple of times, but with no
response. I thought she might have gone out, but I felt a little
worried, so I drove around to the house. I rang the bell, and
when there was no reply, I tried the door; to my amazement it
was unlocked. There was no sign of the maid downstairs, and
when I called, "Carole?" there was no answer. I went upstairs
to the bedroom and it was empty, but the bathroom door was
open, and I saw Carole lying on the floor in a housecoat.

At first I thought she must have fainted, and I went over
and tried to pick her up. My one thought was how I could
bring her back. She was cold, she was gray—to all intents and
purposes she was dead. There was an empty bottle by her side.
I tried everything, holding her, moving her, shouting her
name. I bent down and thought I felt a breath; I tried her
pulse. I couldn't believe she was dead. I had had no experience
with a dead person; during the war I'd seen people wounded
and being carried bleeding out of airplanes, but not a civilian,
with no marks, no outward sign of damage.

I went to the phone beside the bed and there found a little
note to her mother, saying she didn't want to go, but there
was no other way. There was no other note, nothing for me—
I wished there had been, she'd never spoken of her mother,
ever. I was distraught, not for myself, but for Carole. I found
the maid in her room and brought her upstairs and showed
her the body. I asked her to help me find Carole's private

telephone book. It was by the bed, and I went through it. I knew Carole had quite a number of doctors, but she hadn't spoken of them by name; by looking from A to Z, I hoped to find a name I could identify as a doctor's. When I couldn't, I got into my car and drove home as fast as possible to get the telephone number of my own doctor. At this point I still did not fully realize that Carole was past bringing back to life.

My doctor's answering service said he was away, and I remembered then that it was Independence Day. Eventually I reached his assistant, who was downtown and who told me it would take him at least half an hour in the traffic to get back. I didn't know what to do. I rang the Culvers, who also lived in the neighborhood, and asked if they knew a doctor near by. They suggested I ring St. John's Hospital, and also the police, if I thought Carole had taken an overdose, which of course I did. I reported to the hospital and the police that I'd found Carole, and that I hoped she wasn't dead, but that she needed assistance immediately, and I asked them to go right to the house. Then I rang the Culvers to say what I had done, and that I was going back to Carole's house; they kindly offered to come with me.

By the time we got back, the police were there, the fire brigade, everything. I asked the police inspector in charge what had happened, if there was any hope of resuscitating her —I still hoped she could be saved. He inquired who I was, and I explained that I was the man who had rung the police, and gave my name, and said she was a close friend of mine. In quite a kindly way he told me that she had probably been dead at least twelve hours, and that the body had already been taken to the morgue. I never saw her again.

The police questioned me about my movements, and I told them that I had been with Carole the night before until half past nine and had then gone to the Culvers', and how I had found her on the bathroom floor. They said it was a very regrettable suicide; they were satisfied with my explanation and said no further action would be taken, though there would be an autopsy, of course, to establish the cause of death.

I was free to go home. I was completely numb until I got into my own house, when the full enormity of the tragedy hit me, of finding Carole dead, who had been so warm and courageous, and so badly treated by the world in many ways. Why, why, had she done it? After a while I realized that I had to talk to someone. I rang Leland Hayward, and he came over just a few minutes before the press invaded the place. Soon photographers and reporters were swarming into the garden, up the trees, even, some of them, onto the roof.

I refused to see the press. I stayed in the house, and Leland was a tower of strength, taking and sifting telephone calls. I was totally bewildered by the fact that, except for showing a mild concern that I might be going to New York, Carole had given me no warning whatsoever of how she felt. I hadn't realized that she had been many times before at the end of her tether, that there was so little stability in her life, and that, as I learned later, she had already attempted to take her life on previous occasions. She was an enormously sweet person, and a good person, and I was simply knocked over by feeling what a damnable shame it was that such a marvelous girl should be brought to this—not really by our relationship, which was all for the good, but by her background and circumstances catching up on her.

Late at night I managed to get out of the house, undetected, and went to Roland and Nan Culver's. There I was given a small suitcase that had been found just outside a gate in the lane by their house. Carole must have left it there while I was with the Culvers the night she took her life, for it contained the letters I had written to her in London. She had taken them out of the house, evidently, to prevent my being embarrassed by them. It was typical of Carole's sweet nature to act so thoughtfully when she was in such an appalling state of mind. If the press had discovered those letters, what whooping and jubilant screams would have gone up from the Hearst and other newspapers, determined to increase their circulation at the expense of her tragedy.

A doctor was called in to give me a shot, because I was not in the greatest possible shape, and in the morning I woke up to learn that Lilli had read the news in the New York papers and had caught a night flight to Los Angeles. It was loyal of her to return, but then Lilli always has been a very straight person.

The results of the autopsy showed—poor Carole—a considerable amount of alcohol in the blood, together with a great many Seconal barbiturates. There was no doubt that she wanted to die. But the aftermath of her suicide was not what she would have wished. By the next morning it was clear that my friends the columnists, and busybodies and gossips everywhere, were having a field day. Obviously it was a story that would sell newspapers, and the innuendos against me were scarcely credible. There were dark hints of a second note, written to me, which I had destroyed. Without quite saying so, they implied that I had been responsible for Carole's suicide. Perhaps I had jilted her—or provided the pills that had caused her death—or done something even more sinister than that. It was strange that for a society that had turned its back on her while she was alive, Carole had suddenly become a heroine and a betrayed woman. How she would have laughed.

The studio could have given me some support, but as far as I know no statement was made. The atmosphere in the front office was strained, when I went there very much later, and visiting one of the sets I heard someone say, "After all, it happened to Fatty Arbuckle." The comparison with Arbuckle, the outsize comedian of silent films who was implicated in the death of a girl at one of his allegedly orgiastic parties, is fairly indicative of the exaggerated feelings at the time about my personal position. I did not return to the Fox studios for many years.

The police were generally sympathetic, but they had a prob-

"Interrogation" at the Landis inquest (Wide World)

lem in shutting up the newspapers. How or why it was arranged I don't know, but a coroner's inquiry was instituted on
Thursday, July 8. I presume they had to go through the mo-
tions to protect themselves from outside criticism. When I
entered the court that day I was blinded by a bank of flashbulbs, the like of which I'd never seen. There were hundreds
of sightseers leering at me, as if I were in a zoo. Before the
hearing the coroner announced, "There is no question that
Miss Landis's death was suicide." I wondered why, if that was
the case, I had been summoned there to answer questions.

After I'd stepped down, a friend of Carole's, Mrs. Wassen,
testified that she had found a second note, with instructions to
the maid to take the kitten to the vet, because it had a sore

paw. The *Los Angeles Daily News* reported this anticlimactic denouement as follows: "To the consternation and dismay of Hollywood gossips and busybodies, the note apparently failed to mention anything else. The hearing at the Hall of Justice was pretty much a frost."

Carole's funeral was on Saturday, July 10, and before the funeral I went to her house again, with the thought of trying to console her mother. I talked to the poor woman for a long time about Carole: she wasn't hostile, just bewildered. Carole had seen very little of her in recent years, and she couldn't understand the tragedy any more than I could.

I went to the funeral at Forest Lawn. Once again I had to face the ordeal of the blinding flashbulbs—I wondered what Carole would have made of it. I could not bring myself to look at her in her coffin, all made up as her mother had insisted she should be. I sat at the back of the chapel, surrounded by small boys who were chewing gum and reading comics.

[CHAPTER SIX]

The Getting-Up Horse

AFTER that terrible week in July, 1948, I had no great desire to see Hollywood again. Leland Hayward and Maxwell Anderson still wanted me for *Anne of the Thousand Days*— they could not have been more stalwart and encouraging throughout the whole business, and Twentieth Century– Fox agreed to give me leave of absence for the duration of the run of the play.

I had a few weeks before rehearsals started for *Anne* and I was fortunate in that Lilli had a film to do in France with Jean-Pierre Aumont. We flew off to Paris, where we were met by Jean-Pierre. He had brought along his brother-in-law, Jean Roy, who volunteered to take me in hand while Lilli was working in Marseilles.

Jean Roy had been in the Resistance during the war, help- ing to get Allied airmen out of France, and he knew Paris in- timately at many different levels. His gaiety and fun and care- free attitude to life were just the tonic I needed. He didn't give a damn about anything. Though he sensed my despond- ency he wouldn't for a moment allow me to brood; in fact he laughed at my moods. He was my constant companion, and his subsequent death in the Suez war came as a sad shock to me.

Paris and the French were an eye-opener as well as a tonic for me. I found that the French really do have a unique attitude to love, life, and death. Existentialism was in full vogue that summer of 1948, and Jean Roy gave me a fair introduction to a philosophy which was gloriously alien to the standards of Shaw's "middle-class morality." He was deliberately trying to shake me loose from the grip of the angst which I felt.

At the same time I could not escape the feeling that I should have been able to save Carole from destroying herself. Her death was always there in the back of my mind and also the knowledge that very soon I would be facing the grim reality of work, New York, and an unpredictable reception from the American public.

We took an Air France flight to New York which in those days refueled in Iceland. We were about half an hour out of Reykjavik when two of the four engines cut out. We lost height rapidly over the icebergs, and the pilot announced that he was going to try to get back to Iceland. I was frightened as hell by that use of the word "try." To make the landing safer he jettisoned the fuel he had just taken on. Then, after a slow but uneventful landing at Reykjavik, we sat for two days and nights—unthinkable in today's terms—until Air France sent another aircraft to pick us up. We were entertained royally on an American air base and watched the aurora borealis.

When I got back to New York, I had to face financial realities as well. I'd been paid a lot in Hollywood, but had sold our house in Mandeville Canyon at a loss of about thirty thousand dollars, while Collette had been awarded, retroactively, a lump sum of alimony amounting to something like forty thousand dollars. This left me pretty broke. I had enough to go on with for the rehearsal period, and hoped that once I started earning my salary I could keep my head above water.

Maxwell Anderson's *Anne of the Thousand Days* was a com-

With Joyce Redman in *Anne of the Thousand Days*

plicated play, going from the present into the past and back again, stringing flashbacks onto the soliloquies spoken by Henry VIII and by Anne Boleyn. Jo Mielziner was arranging a most intricate series of revolving stages and special chairs in which Anne Boleyn and Henry would be projected into and above the audience when speaking the connecting soliloquies. Bretaigne Windust was directing, Joyce Redman was playing Anne, and we had a very distinguished supporting cast, including Jack Merivale, who became a good friend.

I had a problem of girth to contend with, as I am not precisely the shape of Henry VIII as portrayed by the artists of his time. They made plaster casts of my legs and head so that I could be encased in foam rubber and have beard and cheeks devised to put the head in proportion to the body. Having plaster casts made sounds simple but isn't. The legs are agonizing enough because most of the hairs come away with the plaster, but the head cast is a nightmare. You are walled in with only two straws up your nose to keep you alive, and you sit, breathing slowly through the straws, while the plaster hardens. If you survive, you are eventually rewarded with a death mask of yourself. I found myself thinking what goddamn silly things we have to do in our profession.

The next task was to find the voice and the walk that would fit the size of the man. I used only the lower notes of my vocal range. The walk came easily, simply because I imagined my girth as the audience would see it and took on a heavy man's lumbering gait. I rehearsed in foam rubber and costume, and I studied Holbein's painting of Henry VIII to find the stance and attitude he normally struck.

It was a sizable challenge. We rehearsed all day and sometimes well into the night, refining scenes between Henry and Anne. We were opening in Philadelphia, and we were there when the time came at last to get all the factors together—sets, costumes, and performance. At the dress rehearsal the sets that had sounded so fabulous were finally erected. We started the agonizing business of walking through scenes and doing the changes of scenery and costumes, and nothing worked. We found ourselves having to change costumes in a small section of a revolving stage while it was going around, so that we all became dizzy. As often as not an actor making a bold entrance found himself confronting not the audience but the back wall of the theatre. The soliloquy chairs we had looked forward to so much wouldn't move; the winches that were supposed to project us forward refused to function. It was one of the most chaotic and depressing evenings of my life.

By the time we broke up, about four o'clock in the morning, it had been decided to postpone the opening by one day. We would try again, after we had snatched some sleep. The next day we battled once more with the revolving stage and the moving chairs, with the same results. The fact had to be faced: there were about twenty changes during the action for which the sets were simply impracticable. The drastic decision was taken to postpone for ten days and scrap the whole decor. Mielziner was to go back to New York and design a Tudor-esque shape with playing areas which, with lighting, it was hoped the audience would imagine to be both exterior and interior.

At this point my digestive system collapsed. I went to a doctor and had X rays taken, which I understand are still being shown to medical students in Philadelphia as examples of what intestines can do under duress. They were in knots—bowlines and hitches. I carried on, relaxing as much as I could with Scotch, which only made the knots tighter, and we continued rehearsing in an empty theatre. The box office was going mad returning money to customers and trying to alter the opening dates to coincide with the date when we thought we would be ready.

It was about this time, waiting nervously for the opening, that I gave an interview to a Philadelphia newspaper blasting Hollywood and its gossip columnists. It was picked up everywhere and made a lot of space. The columnists didn't know what to do. Louella Parsons got on the air and made the statement, "Rex Harrison says we're a lot of old sex-starved columnists," which brought hoots of laughter from all but the squares. They decided the way to deal with me was never to mention my name again. This suited me down to the ground. Other people said when they'd read the interview that they hoped I realized what I had done, that I'd never be able to go back to Hollywood again. That was fine by me. My digestion improved miraculously.

We waited impatiently for Jo Mielziner's new set, with poor Leland Hayward going grayer and grayer, brooding over how much money he was losing. It was a nerve-racking time. But when the set arrived, it was a lovely dark-green velvet Tudor shape, with steps leading down to the stage level, nice to act on, lovely to look at, a background against which the costumes stood out brilliantly. Joyce Redman and I had what they call follow spots, which are mostly used in musical comedy; in this instance they could be reduced to a mere pinpoint, so that only the actor's head was visible in the dark. The whole design worked like a dream. We forgot about those magic soliloquy chairs and sat in a pool of light—much more effective. The only pity was that we hadn't started out that way.

We played two weeks in Philadelphia and found that the play lagged at times. Cuts were made, and Maxwell Anderson was locked up in his hotel room rewriting scenes which we rehearsed during the day, while playing at night. We booked a further two weeks away from New York, in Baltimore, postponing our opening at the Shubert Theatre. Another large expense, but Leland had fantastic tenacity and was determined to get it right. In Baltimore the play began to settle down and work. I was amazed too by the warmth the audience showed toward me. I had had no idea what my reception would be, after all that had been written about me after Carole's suicide.

We opened at the Shubert in New York in early December, and the play was acclaimed by all the critics as a masterpiece.

I won the Best Actor of the Year, the Antoinette Perry, Award, and it was presented to me at the Waldorf-Astoria Hotel in the presence of at least one of the "old sex-starved columnists," Hedda Hopper, who had said, before she stopped mentioning my name, "Rex Harrison is deader than a dead mackerel." The strange independence of public opinion was manifested by seething mobs of people waiting outside the stage door in Shubert Alley, all wishing me luck and clapping; sometimes the public makes up its own mind about what it reads. The play ran for about six months until we laid off for the summer, as was the custom of that period before air conditioning.

While I was on tour Lilli had occupied herself with trying to find a place to live in New York, and after the opening we took a flat, an inexpensive place on the fifteenth floor of one of the big blocks of apartments on Central Park West. Our relationship since our return from Paris had remained uneasy. For a while after coming back to me, Lilli had felt she was doing the right thing, the correct thing, and she had been wonderful. As time went on, recriminations naturally set in. I don't blame her at all, but it made life extremely uneasy and unhappy. Still, we struggled on. I was in financial difficulties; I was paying for the flat and expenses out of my weekly salary, which was 10 percent of the Shubert Theatre's gross, and each week everything went out that came in.

I managed to save a little, however, just enough for us to decide that we would take a break before the play reopened on September 1. We hoped that perhaps a holiday would do us both good. Lilli's friend Dr. Rolf Gerard suggested Santa Margherita, saying that it was not expensive, and we followed up his idea. We thought it might be fun to have friends with us, so we asked Jack Merivale and Sally Cooper, Gladys Cooper's daughter, if they would come.

In Santa Margherita we stayed in a hotel called the Miramar. We found the place very pretty, and we used to take an outboard motorboat, with a man called Alberto, out along the coast or around to Portofino, returning to our hotel to eat, because none of us had very much money. I think I fell in love with the village of Portofino at first sight, especially seeing it while coming in from the sea.

I went over there one day with Alberto. We found a mule track at the back of the port and climbed to the very top of the hill. There I sat down to rest, and found I could see the whole coast of Liguria, right down to La Spezia. Below me was the port, which had been used by the Crusaders, down the coast the Apennines were running, rising out of the water were Chiavari, Sestri Levante, and a marvelous part of the world called the Cinque Terre, which means the Five Hills, five little villages all stuck on rocks, with a castle to defend them, which among them manage to produce quite a lot of wine.

I sat looking at this splendor, just gazed and gloried in it, and in the unkempt hillside, terraced long ago, and in its olive trees, most of them uncared for, with a lot of lichen on the bark. I thought I'd never seen anything like it.

And so it was that I found my plot of land above Portofino and found that it was for sale. As I was going to Rome to discuss a film for which I would be paid partly in lire, I gambled my all and bought it; the film fell through, but by a stroke of luck was replaced by another, and the lovely house that I built still stands there on the hill above Portofino. It has seen many twists of fortune, but is none the worse for that.

Lilli and I went back to New York, and I reopened the next season at the Shubert. We had a good run for about four months, then business started to taper off. But Leland had lost so much money on the opening that I went on tour with the play through the Middle West and Canada.

The film which paid for my Portofino venture was called *The Long Dark Hall* and I must say, to my shame, I hardly asked to see the script. I had to see it, eventually, and then discovered that I was playing a suburban murderer, living in a dingy terraced house in some Midland town. Not the sort of role I'm accustomed to playing; though if anybody could find the negative of that film, it might be very much in vogue. It was one of the worst pictures I've ever made, but luckily I don't think anybody saw it. By now we were in the new year of 1950, and it was arranged that the film would be made in the summer. Lilli, while I was on the road, had been playing in *Caesar and Cleopatra* with Cedric Hardwicke. The play was a success and was still running, when I had an offer to do T. S. Eliot's *The Cocktail Party* in England.

I had previously been approached by Richard Rodgers and Oscar Hammerstein to do the musical version of the film *Anna and the King of Siam,* which was to be called *The King and I.* I was very honored, and also, obviously, torn, partly because I had yet to do *The Long Dark Hall,* and partly because I wanted to try my hand at this marvelous play of Eliot's, which I had seen Alec Guinness playing in New York. It's strange to think that if I hadn't gone on that holiday to Santa Margherita, if I hadn't found that plot of land and committed myself to *The Long Dark Hall* for financial reasons, I might have chosen *The King and I,* stayed with it for five years, and gone on to do the film. I might never have done *My Fair Lady,* and I would now be known as the man with dozens of wives and ninety children, rather than as an irascible misogynist. As it is, Yul Brynner did *The King and I,* which turned out to be a record-breaking musical if ever there was one, and he was magnificent. When he opened I sent him a telegram saying, "The King is dead, long live the King." It is extraordinary, the roads taken and not taken.

The Cocktail Party intrigued me enormously. I got on to one of the *Queens* and started to work on the play, trying as we steamed across the Atlantic to get my tongue around Eliot's extremely complicated blank verse. In London I found that Margaret Leighton was playing Celia, and we started to rehearse with a superb cast.

Playwrights are an interesting breed, and I have always loved them for their perseverance and skill, and for their generosity in being able to hand over the newborn babe for

In *The Cocktail Party* (Anthony Buckley)

the directors and actors to put life into it. There is nothing stiller than the stillborn page of an unplayed play, and the fascination of acting and directing lies in taking this material and making it live, giving it dimensions. And if it is important for directors and actors to choose material suited to their talents, it is vital that the playwright, who lives the play as he writes it, should not become disillusioned if sometimes it does not come out quite as he saw it in his mind. Tom Eliot came regularly to rehearsals and would carefully consider our difficulties and suggestions.

It had been agreed that I'd do the play for three months only, because I had this film commitment. We opened in Southsea, and then in London, in May. Eliot and the play got extremely good notices, but what I hadn't taken into account, because I was in America, was that before the opening in New York it had played at the Edinburgh Festival with Alec Guinness and had been critically noticed at that time. The *Daily Telegraph,* wishing to be funny, or clever, or correct, and no doubt meaning every word of it, came out with the verdict, "Mine's a Guinness," a quip borrowed from a very popular poster of the time advertising Guinness stout. Luckily all the critics didn't take that view.

The Cocktail Party is a brilliant and difficult play—at the end of each performance the audience would sit numb and silent for quite a time, before breaking into applause, and after they had filed out I used to go back to my dressing room and stare at myself in the mirror, feeling that I'd been sitting for several hours in a tepid bath. Eliot's writing was cerebral and unemotional. But the theme of the play, in which Eliot points up how people in great mental anguish will find "guardians"—those who have already been through the fire and endured—to help them over bad times, I believe is absolutely true. I have often seen it in my lifetime: I have had guardians and have been a guardian.

In the play I was the Unidentified Guest, the doctor, whose principal concern as guardian is with a girl called Celia who is in love with a married man. He counsels her to obey her own impulse and go abroad and find hard and useful work, perhaps in a missionary capacity; and when Celia obeys him and dies a frightening death at the hands of the people she has been helping, he sees this not as failure, but as the fulfillment of her identity.

At the end of the second act, when the guardians gather around to drink a libation to Celia, I had to pour the port out of a decanter. Being partially blind in one eye, I failed on one occasion to notice that the stage manager had left the glasses upside down. I went on pouring, saying Eliot's complicated blank-verse patterns, and suddenly realized to my horror that the port was going over the tray and over my desk, and that I had been pouring it onto the stems. I righted the glasses and mopped up the desk with my handkerchief, and all the while the audience sat as quiet as mice, thinking I'm sure that it was all part of Eliot's metaphysical overtones.

I remember Vivien Leigh was extremely fond of the play and came to see it several times. One day at a matinee I had a slight cramp in my left hand, and during the scene with Celia I cracked a joint. Vivien came around afterward, as she always did, and said, "That was absolutely marvelous, that cracking of the joint—what did that mean? It must have meant something?" I said it didn't mean anything, it meant that I'd got cramp in my left hand. But it was that sort of play, it held people spellbound.

Margaret Leighton did it for two months, and then I was joined by Irene Worth, who'd played Celia in Edinburgh and New York. It was an interesting experience, to play opposite two actresses with such very different acting styles. Margaret Leighton's was very realistic, as was mine, while Irene Worth tried for an abstract note, which I assumed was in the style of the Guinness production.

Lilli finished her run in New York and joined me in London, where we found that things were getting a little bit easier between us. Time had healed a few of her miseries and some of my unhappiness. We then did *The Long Dark Hall,* which took about eight weeks, and by the time we received payment for this film, the villa in Portofino was more than half finished.

On the strength of her performance as Cleopatra, Lilli was asked to play in New York again, in John Van Druten's *Bell, Book and Candle.* I was by then working on a play called *The Next Lord Chase,* which I was trying to get ready for presentation in England. As the date drew near for rehearsals to start, the right leading man had still not been found for Lilli's play, while I found I was getting nowhere with my play; so I called Irene Selznick, the producer, and asked if I could play opposite Lilli for a limited run of three months. Irene said that she was of course delighted with the idea, and so Lilli and I went to New York and began to rehearse.

Bell, Book and Candle was an enormous success, it ran and ran and ran, and when we closed we were still doing big business. I was later to do it in London, directing it and playing in it.

As the season drew to its close at the end of May, 1951, I grew more and more excited about seeing the villa, which was now completed. We had been down for a couple of days, but then the villa had been little more than a shell. I enjoyed seeing how the Italians build their houses, blasting the rock from the hill and building the house like a jigsaw puzzle as they chip the rocks into shape and fit them together, making the walls like the old dry-stone walls between fields.

I was particularly pleased with the position of the house. I wasn't allowed to build it near the top of the hill, because they don't like things showing against the skyline when seen from the sea, and so we had tucked it into the hill, just below the crest, and built it on two wings, like a pushed-out V. It's since become beautifully overgrown with bougainvillea and grapes and is very hard to pick out from the sea.

Although I wasn't able to spend a lot of money on the house, labor was not nearly as expensive then as it is now, so that what money there was went quite a long way. It isn't a luxuri-

Portofino

ous house, but it's comfortable, and it is the view that makes it. We spent a good summer there, and I felt it had given me a new lease of some kind. I had quite a bit of land, which hadn't been developed at all then, it was very rough, and it was marvelous to wander about, planning how to terrace it and put in vineyards and lay out the different gardens.

After the summer I went back to London, with nothing planned for the future; having left *Bell, Book and Candle* with a fairly full house at the Ethel Barrymore Theatre, I found myself without work and again without very much money. Laurence Olivier had a lease then on the St. James's Theatre, where he was playing Shaw's *Caesar and Cleopatra* and Shakespeare's *Antony and Cleopatra,* but he was planning to go to New York to direct a season of plays. He asked me if I'd like to play there in Christopher Fry's *Venus Observed,* in the part he himself had played in London, with Lilli playing the leading lady. Naturally I was thrilled by the idea, especially as Fry was another new venture for me, and a sharp contrast to Eliot. Eliot's blank verse was wonderfully worked, with every word weighed, and used to make an exact point, sparse and dry; Fry was immensely lyrical, using a splendid diversity of rich images. I very much enjoyed these modern verse plays.

Larry and I got on splendidly. I'd never worked with him before, and now I found him a marvelous director. It wasn't easy for him, considering that he'd played the part himself in London, and it wasn't easy for me, but he gave me a great deal of help. He must have been exhausted by the end, because Vivien wasn't well, and on top of that he was playing eight shows a week as well as directing.

They brought over the set of Roger Furse's that they'd used at the St. James's, hoping to find a small theatre, but the Shuberts insisted on putting us in the New Century Theatre, an enormous theatre on Seventh Avenue below Central Park South totally unsuited to a very intimate, complex verse play. Larry and I went to see Lee Shubert to explain our point of view, but we got nowhere at all and were obliged to try to put the play across in a place like the Colosseum. It was a desperate battle. There was no way of reaching the back of the theatre with that sort of strange, marvelous, firework display of words. The words made great patterns, but you had to say them delicately; they couldn't be forced out into a big auditorium.

By this time I was so absorbed in the theatre that Beverly Hills and the columnists and the studios seemed to belong to another world. We bought on mortgage a small flat on the East River near Gracie Square, in the eighties, thinking it better, since I was going to spend quite a lot of my life in New York, to buy an apartment rather than to keep renting. I spent my days exercising, around the park and up and down the promenade along the river, getting the brilliant air off the river into my lungs so that I could get my tongue around Fry's tongue twisters at night.

Venus Observed opened in February, 1952, and closed I think in April. In May, Lilli and I went out to Hollywood to do *The Fourposter*. It didn't really work, from the filming point of view. We rehearsed for three weeks, mapping it out and learning it, while the cameraman wandered about to see what we were doing; but rehearsing camera setups isn't like rehearsing a play. Camera setups take a long time and are done in small sections, and by the end of the three weeks, of course, we had forgotten what we'd rehearsed at the beginning. We then had only two weeks for shooting, and I quite soon got lost, because I hadn't the time to prepare. It was a horrible experience for me, though I think the film was quite well liked.

It was four years since I had left, but Hollywood didn't seem to have changed. It was not until a few years later that the latent jealousy between theatre and film actors came into the open; in the early Sixties theatre actors looked down on films—because they weren't asked to play in them—and the film industry began to wane. In 1952 the Hollywood monopoly still looked as strong as ever.

At the end of June we went off to Portofino again. The house was finished by then, and our first visitors were our friends from California, Roland and Nan Culver. Lilli was good with the local Italians and it was a very gay and social summer. That was the year of the yachts, when the Windsors came to Portofino, and we had a stream of people calling on us when they came into port.

One of the yachts brought Garbo to stay with us at the villa. Whenever she appeared in the port, en route between her yacht and the villa, the locals, instead of clamoring for autographs, used quite simply to stand and applaud. She would hurry across the piazza, trying to hide herself, and they would stand and clap, which I've never seen before or since. It is quite true, she really does want to be alone, and she doesn't want to be stared at. She is an extraordinarily attractive person, and very shy and very Nordic—very depressed. She loved to walk, undisturbed, up the tracks to the farms beyond our house, and sometimes I went with her. I loved talking to her. She had great moments of gaiety—in an evening, she could be scintillating for hours on end, and then she'd go back into a deep depression.

The Duke of Windsor, who was in harbor at the time, had never met Garbo, so we were bidden to go on board with her, and it was a very odd evening. From time to time during dinner the conversation got a bit tricky, because there were a number of exceptionally right-wing businessmen in the party, and some of us didn't altogether agree with their theories. When trouble threatened, Jimmy Donahue, a friend of the Duchess's, simply jumped overboard in all his clothes. This caused a diversion, while everyone went to the rail. He did a full change, came back, and when things once more got a bit sticky jumped straight into the port again. The Duke of Windsor became particularly fond of Lilli, and they used to get together to sing German songs, which he enjoyed very much.

I remember too standing on the roof garden of the villa while John Gielgud explained to me the classical method of speaking Tudor verse, which I'd never conquered. Gielgud said he pushed emotion through the speech, without necessarily thinking of the words he was saying and making every word clear, whereas it had been my whole training to clarify the meaning of each speech.

While Noël Coward and Graham Payn were staying with us Lilli and I had to go to the Venice Festival, so we left them there, and they kept house for us. When we came back they'd done some lovely paintings of the port as seen from the villa.

Another constant visitor to the villa who was a great joy to us was Jean-Pierre Aumont. He had not long before lost his wife, Maria Montez, the film star and a great South American beauty. She had been in the habit of taking very hot baths so as to lose weight, and one day she must have fainted in the bath, and drowned. Jean-Pierre was at the studio when they told him, and though he got back as fast as he could and tried to get the fire brigade and anyone else he could to resuscitate her, she'd gone. He took a long time to recover from her death.

John and Mary Mills also came to stay with us, then and in subsequent years. While he was down there, John made films in eight-millimeter, in which he always played the comic.

It was Max Beerbohm who suggested to us a name for the villa. One day when I was visiting him in Rapallo, he said, "Why don't you call your villa San Genesio?" San Genesio is almost unknown even to Italians, but he's the patron saint of actors, something that Max would know about. The legend has it that Genesio was a comic mime, who liked to do a take-off on the Holy Sacrament for the delight of unbelievers. One day during this performance he had a true vision of Christ, became a believer, and was promptly executed by the unbelievers. He was later canonized. San Genesio's Day, I found, is in August, and though the Italians may not have heard of him, he does exist—or did. It would take someone of Max's sweetness to have thought of such an illustrious name for my strange folly.

Perhaps too much has been said about the ways in which actors ease the pressures—loving, drinking, talking, whatever. But in order to interpret characters under emotional stress we must necessarily have a lot of varied emotions bottled up within ourselves; and there is also the nagging feeling, always, if you haven't got work to go to, what *are* you going to do? Though I found that San Genesio was the nearest I could get in those days to a place of peace, even there I ended up feeling restless after a while. I didn't have anything planned for the winter, and again, although we were living quite well, there was not a lot in the coffers.

The Theatre Guild of New York came to my rescue by asking if I would like to act in and direct Peter Ustinov's *The Love of Four Colonels*. I was very excited by the idea of directing, for the first time, though I didn't realize then how difficult it is to try to direct while acting in the play as well. I said I'd go and see the play in London and then let them know.

I left Portofino for London in the late summer, and liked the play enormously, although I thought it was a little long. Peter Ustinov was marvelously funny in it and the whole concept, with its parodies of Chekhov, Shakespeare, Restoration comedy, and modern American drama, was strikingly original. I told the Theatre Guild that I'd very much like to do it, and left for New York to start work on the play, doing a little editing and preparing for the production. Robert Coote, my friend of many decades, I got to play the English colonel; and I asked Dr. Rolf Gerard, who had been working at the Metropolitan Opera and had done some excellent sets there, to do the rather elaborate settings needed for the Ustinov play.

The play, which is about an English, an American, a French, and a Russian colonel in a small hut in occupied Europe, tempted by a wicked fairy to follow him into the woods, where they will each have the chance to make love to a fairy princess, was a great success at the Shubert Theatre. I managed to combine directing with acting, and it had a good run, from January to the usual end of May. Ustinov won the Best Foreign Play of the Year Award.

While we were playing in Boston, I gave up smoking. That was in 1953, so I haven't smoked now for more than twenty years. I was then smoking some six or seven packets a day—I never finished a cigarette, but I was never without one in my hand. When I complained to the doctor that I felt terrible and couldn't even feel my nerve ends, he said, "You've got nicotine poisoning. If you want to put years on your life, give it up."

It was a struggle, but I switched to cigars, and stopped inhaling, and then slowly gave up the cigars. It took about six months.

When the play closed the pattern now of course was to go down to Portofino for the summer. I had Robert Coote and Jack Merivale down to stay with me; they were a marvelous buffer against the social life, which was beginning to wear me down. I didn't like very large dinner parties where Italian was spoken most of the time; Lilli, of course, being a brilliant linguist, speaking German and English and Italian, had a great time, but I needed a little buffer, and these two friends of mine provided me with a change of pace. They both enjoyed the good things in life, but not necessarily in such a social milieu. The three of us would go off to the port, drink far too much, and laugh a lot, it was all very impromptu. Then we'd go back to the villa for a circumspect dinner. Since Lilli didn't drink and was no companion to those who did, I tended always to invite friends of a cheerful disposition to stay.

Back again in New York in September, we reopened *The Love of Four Colonels,* but it had run its course there really, and after a month or so in the Shubert we took it out on the road, as I had done with *Anne of the Thousand Days.* I remember we opened the tour in a strange town which smelled only of chocolate—Hershey, Pennsylvania, the original chocolate-bar factory town. The tour didn't last very long, and while we were in Detroit, where the play finally closed, I received to my surprise yet another offer from Hollywood.

These little offers that came along had been completely disregarded by the columnists. When I'd gone back there to do *The Fourposter,* they'd kept their promise not to write anything about me, which was fine by me. Now I went back to do an adaptation of *The Talisman,* the novel by Sir Walter Scott. They called it *King Richard and the Crusaders,* and it was made at Warner Brothers. Jack Warner was the brave soul who asked me to do it, who cared no more than I did for the dictates of the Hollywood press and pacemakers. His sense of the ridiculous was very acute.

King Richard and the Crusaders was an absolutely rotten picture, almost the last of its kind. King Richard was played by George Sanders, Laurence Harvey played the juvenile, and I was Saladin, King of the Saracens. For this part I was blacked up, for the first time since I'd climbed that tree back at the Playhouse; luckily there were no trees to climb on this occasion, and anyway I'd learned a bit more about the art of staying black.

It was the first horsy film I'd played in, and I was fascinated. I had to fight lots of duels on horseback, and get knocked off my horse, and climb back on, and execute all those other marvelous maneuvers that I'd seen other people do. I learned that there's a creature called a Falling-Down Horse, and another called a Getting-Up Horse, who must look alike. The Falling-Down Horse has been so trained that at the slightest pressure from the rider's leg it will topple over in such a way that the rider can throw himself free, as he goes over, without damaging the horse or himself. The film then cuts away to another piece of action and a little while later comes back to find the rider lying on the ground beside a horse—apparently the same horse, but this time it's the Getting-Up Horse, tethered with invisible wires. The moment the rider approaches it and puts his leg over it, the wires are let go and the horse stands up. It looks absolutely stunning and it's the easiest thing in the world. There are also a Rearing Horse and a Bucking Horse, which are brought on like special acts.

The other thing I learned about was the jousting, and its very careful timing. They attach a wire to the garment of the actor who's going to fall off, and the moment the lance comes within a couple of inches of his breastplate, he's yanked off backward on the end of the wire. This, of course, is an expert's stunt, done with doubles. I was fascinated to watch all those technical feats, which we didn't do in England.

131

I felt a little bit better this time about being back in Holly-wood. I was no longer in Beverly Hills, because the Warner Brothers studio is in the San Fernando Valley, on the other side of the hills, and in a way it has a different atmosphere. I thought I'd indulge myself by taking Errol Flynn's house. Errol Flynn had left it ages ago, and had left Hollywood—he was somewhere on his yacht—but the house was still to be had, so I took it, even if I couldn't afford it. It was a splendid house, a relic of the old days, with great signs of Flynn at his most elaborate and bizarre. It had a tennis court, a big work-room, and it was full of steam baths and two-way mirrors, tape machines in every bedroom, all the gadgets that Flynn enjoyed, and all rather ramshackle.

While there I had a letter from Sidney Gilliat, with whom I'd made *The Rake's Progress* at the end of the war, saying that he had written another film and hoped to have me act in it. It was intended as a kind of counterpart to *The Rake's Progress,* and he'd called it *Marriage à la Mode,* a marvelous title. But Sidney seemed fated to have trouble with the dis-tributors over his titles. Just as *The Rake's Progress* had be-come, in America, *Notorious Gentleman,* so *Marriage à la Mode,* which the distributors thought might be an ice cream topped with cherries, but certainly not anything else, became *The Constant Husband,* which is a less than marvelous title.

It was about a man who has had a car accident and is suffer-ing from amnesia, finding that he is married to no less than six women.

I told Sidney that I thought the idea was splendid, and he wrote back saying that he hoped if I did it I would take a hand in the casting too, but that he had cast one part with a very up-and-coming young actress named Kay Kendall.

CHAPTER SEVEN

Kay

My first encounter with Kay Kendall was over lunch at the studios in England, perhaps a week before the filming started of *The Constant Husband,* in the spring of 1954. She was very easy, full of fun, beautifully inconsequential, flirtatious, impertinent, and rakish. I felt instinctively that here was a unique sad-gay sprite, adrift, yet clearly totally at home even in that drab cafeteria.

Lilli had left to make a film in Munich called *Feuerwerk,* a Swiss-German musical, and I was alone in London when the time came to begin filming *The Constant Husband.* There were three leading ladies, Margaret Leighton, Nicole Maurey, and Kay, so that, although I was working every day, there were long gaps when Kay was not called, and as soon as her work was done she would always leave that same evening for Paris. This was very frustrating. Having been quite bowled over, I wanted to see more and more of her.

I felt strangely desolated whenever she disappeared. It was frightening that somebody I knew only superficially should have such a violent effect on me. It was like a light going out in the room when she left.

Before many weeks her visits to Paris became a little less

frequent. I never asked why, but we began seeing more of each other. Perhaps she began to care for me. As we started to know each other better, and acquaintance ripened into close friendship, her vitality and magical joy in living infected me as nothing had ever done before.

She showed me bits of London I'd never seen—she was a true Cockney, and she loved her city. She made it seem like a village and most particularly her village. She had lived through the blitz in St. Martin's Lane, over a pub called the Salisbury, with her mother and sister, and later had bicycled every night to work at the Palladium, where she was in the chorus. She had grown up in the area of Covent Garden and knew every lane and byway of that warren. We used to roam through the small streets, stopping at coffee stalls when we felt hungry.

She started another film after she had done her bit in *The Constant Husband*. We used to meet at night, sometimes going to hear my elder son, Noel, play the guitar at a dive called Esmeralda's Barn. Lilli was still making her long German musical, and I was staying at a hotel, but Kay moved constantly from one furnished flat to another. She must have had at least four flats during this period. She would take them by the week and not like them, and more often than not move into something I thought was far worse. She always went to extremes, it seemed: totally broke, frozen stiff in the cold, always wearing clothes quite unsuited to the weather.

Great battles, fisticuffs, runnings away, reconciliations, and an incessant hectic activity filled her mad life. She was always funny, even when doing the most impossibly stupid things, which indeed she never stopped doing. She was twenty-six then (I was forty-six), and it was as if some demon was driving her to live recklessly, almost dottily. She was of course a clown above all—this was her irresistible charm. It was not for nothing that she was half Irish. Kay Kendall MacCarthy was her full name; maybe that MacCarthy did it.

The idyll ended, as we thought, with the completion of

Kay and Rex

The Constant Husband. In total agony, not knowing what I would do or how I would live, I left London to join Lilli in Munich.

I was dead. How I stuck out those days in Munich I shall never know. There is something about the German accent that gives me goose pimples—perhaps a nurse had threatened, with a bad imitation of the accent, to turn me over to the Germans if I was naughty. Now Lilli was making a German-language film, and there was no escape from it. All I could think of was how to get to a telephone to call Kay.

At last it was time to leave Munich and drive down to Portofino for the summer. I struggled on, fighting the urge to be by Kay's side, an urge that was almost like a disease. I could not rid myself of it. It was not just a physical need, but a desire to be together—to laugh, to protect, to talk.

After a week in Portofino a lucky chance came up to visit London, because Carey had to be collected from his prep school at Sunningdale and brought back to the villa. Kay and I met the day I arrived back. I realized I had fallen deeply in love. How deep her affections were for me I wasn't sure, although beneath her jokes and fun I felt that she desperately needed care and love, and knew now that she was getting both.

We had only a few days, and then I left with Carey for Portofino, while Kay went off on a holiday to St.-Jean-de-Luz, near Biarritz. We both felt there was no future for us, and I was torn by a sense of loyalty to Lilli and my son. We said good-bye forever.

Back at the villa in Portofino I found a cheerful house party, with Larry Olivier and Vivien and Jean-Pierre Aumont as guests. I tried to enter into the fun. Kay had disappeared: it had been good-bye, and I had no idea where she was staying in France. I had a contract to start rehearsing the London production of *Bell, Book and Candle,* when the holidays were over, with my wife. That was that. I would get over it—I would have to get over it.

I was having dinner in the port at a restaurant called Pitosfero with a very social group, including the Duke and Duchess of Windsor, when a message came saying that I was wanted urgently, if I could leave for a minute without disturbing the dinner party. I excused myself to the Duke and Duchess, wondering what it could possibly be. It was Kay, waiting for me at a café in the port. I was elated, and also extremely apprehensive.

It was typical of Kay, to do something like this and then pretend to me that it was all a coincidence, that she'd been "passing by." She had arranged it all, but she was damned if she was going to admit it to me then. She knew she shouldn't have done it, but she couldn't help herself, any more than I could.

We had a quick drink and arranged to meet early the next morning, and I returned to the restaurant, to be given some very dubious regal looks from His Royal Highness.

Next morning, bright and early, I left the villa in the Jeep and drove over to Santa Margherita, where Kay was staying at the Hotel Eden, and asked Kay and Carol Saroyan, William Saroyan's wife, to come over and spend the afternoon on a yacht belonging to the Earl of Warwick, and afterward to come to dinner at the villa. Carol Saroyan had been in on Kay's plot from the beginning, of course, but was still very nervous about the whole thing.

Carol was quite right to be nervous. The yacht expedition and the dinner party were both disastrous. Kay and I were too obviously in love to be anything but embarrassing to anyone else, and Lilli had every reason to be both upset and cross. The evening ended icily.

I don't quite know where we would have gone from there if the next day Carol Saroyan had not come down with acute appendicitis. She was taken to the Rapallo clinic, and Kay had to leave for Switzerland to pick up some clothes for her. But before she left she managed to get a message up to the villa. I went out and telephoned her, and we arranged to meet in Milan.

This was the first overt and premeditated step I had taken in my romance with Kay. The film, the visit to London, were part of the prescribed order of events; Kay's arrival in Porto-fino was her own declaration of intent; going to Milan was mine. To begin with I was in a state of shock at what I was doing. I had left the villa, driven the Jeep to the gate, and got into my car, with no good-byes—no explanations. I was pulled in two directions, and can remember the two and a half hours' drive to this day. I don't think anything could have stopped me from going, short of a head-on collision, and yet I had a constant urge to turn back.

We stayed away together for a week. We put the top down on my old Jaguar and drove up into the Apennines—we didn't want cities. We had frightful problems in finding accommoda-tion, it being the height of the season, and I remember we both quite solemnly considered spending a night at a farm-house that had a sort of large dog's bed under the table in the front room. Finally we were driven back from the mountains into the cities just to get a good night's rest.

Katie fell in love with Genoa, the old thirteenth-century town with narrow streets lined with towers, so that they feel like canyons. We ate in little cafés and wandered through the labyrinthine streets, sometimes just following people to see where they would end up. I particularly remember walking along behind one old couple who were having the most tre-mendous verbal battle, the violence of which reminded us so much of ourselves it made us laugh. It was so endearing, because they must both have been about eighty, and when they arrived at their little house they went quite quietly in together. Rows in Italian, especially in a Genoese accent, sound wonderful.

Finally Kay had to go back to Carol, who was recovering from her operation in Rapallo, and take her to Switzerland, and I felt I had to return to the villa, at least to get some clothes and make a plan.

Carcy and the nanny were still at the villa, but Lilli I found had, not unnaturally, left for London. Come hell or high water, I was committed to doing *Bell, Book and Candle* with her in September, but I decided in the meantime to go and spend a week or two with Jean-Pierre Aumont, who had a house outside Paris on the Malmaison estate.

I was quite lost without Kay and called her from there. When she came to the phone she told me the maid had said somebody was ringing her from the Bad House. She said, "What the hell d'you think you're doing at the Bad House?" I explained about the Malmaison estate, and she said she was catching the next train.

We had a lovely week in Paris, doing a lot of mad things and having fun. Kay and I were alike in that every day, every meal, every minute had to be made the most of. If I thought I had energy, God, she had double. The time flew by, dogged by the dread of the return to reality, until I had to go back and face the music.

Those were grim days, for I was directing as well as acting in *Bell, Book and Candle,* and naturally the relationship with Lilli was very strained. We plodded through a production of froth and bubbles with heavy hearts. It must have been agony for Lilli and I could not escape the fact that I was responsible for it.

We toured, and opened in the West End at the Phoenix Theatre, ironically enough to rave notices. Even more ironic was the applause for an apparently devoted husband-and-wife partnership, smiling and bowing to each other through the din of clapping.

I had never done things by halves, and yet now my heart was divided. It would not mend for wanting Kay, but at the same time I was bitterly unhappy for Lilli, who had done nothing to deserve her plight.

We parted: Lilli moved to a flat. I stayed on at my hotel, determined not to move anywhere. I did not want to make any final or decisive move. But shortly after she took her flat, Lilli found herself an old friend from Hollywood and South America, Carlos Thompson, to whom she is now married.

To add to my problems, Hugh Beaumont now offered me the direction of another play, called *Nina,* at the same time as I was playing *Bell, Book and Candle.* He was extremely fond of Lilli, I know, and in the kindest possible way he must have thought that by keeping me busy he might help to take my mind off my private affairs, and even, perhaps, off Kay.

Nina was written by André Roussin, a great exponent of boulevard comedy; it was a three-handed play in the traditional mold, with a woman, a husband, and a lover. In Paris the part of Nina Tessier had been played by the great Romanian actress Popescu, and in London it was going to be played by Dame Edith Evans. The prospect of directing this marvelous actress, whose work I'd always admired, was very exciting.

It was not easy to cast the other two parts. Hugh Beaumont and I searched around and eventually settled for Charles Goldner in the role of the lover, Georges de Fourville, and James Hayter in the role of the husband, Adolphe. James Hayter was a great favorite with the management, so I agreed to try him.

Charles Goldner, however, had been in the hospital and was not well. We had a reading at Hugh Beaumont's house, at which Goldner read his part beautifully; a week later he went back into the hospital, and within ten days he was dead. Naturally we were all very upset, and all our plans had to be changed. Eventually we decided that Dame Edith should at least meet David Hutcheson so that we could see what she thought of him. He was a tall, attractive, and funny actor, and Dame Edith liked him on first meeting, so he and Dame Edith and Hayter started at last to rehearse, under my direction, at the Haymarket.

With the permission of the management, H. M. Tennent, I got my old friend Arthur Barbosa to do the décor. Arthur did me a very pretty French set, but I in my idiocy didn't like it. I remembered a set I had seen ages ago in *By Candle Light* and thought that was the kind of set we needed. I found a picture of it and got Arthur to put together a very hot, draped room, with a bed covered in furs and all that sort of stuff, for the lovers' scene. I thought it would be very sexy, and in fact it was a disaster.

It soon became clear too that Dame Edith was extremely uncomfortable, not with herself, but with the supporting cast. Hayter and Hutcheson hadn't the experience and the extraordinarily fine intelligence that Dame Edith brings to all her parts, and she did not know how to adjust to their styles of acting. As it was a three-handed play, she was always playing a scene with one or the other, and she became more and more unhappy. If I went up on the stage to demonstrate a scene with her, she became a different person, and she said, "If only I could play it with you, it would be so different." I had to point out that I was playing at the Phoenix, and couldn't do it. There was nothing I could do except work on the other two actors, and that meant leaving Dame Edith sitting about waiting too long for her entrances. I too became quite desperate with her unhappiness, and on one occasion when Dame Edith got dreadfully upset I took her down into the stalls, sat there with my arm around her, and asked her if she would take one of my pills. I was at that time always covered in pills, and this one was a sort of long-playing phenobarbital pill, full of little bombs that went off at timed intervals. Dame Edith is a Christian Scientist, and I think that was probably the first and last pill she ever took, and then only out of sheer desperation.

We struggled on with the rehearsals, and she seemed to be settling down. In spite of our problems, it was wonderful working with her, seeing her map out long speeches and color them with moves, watching the way she caught the light with angles of her face and head, and I shall always be grateful that I was able to sit in the audience and watch such a fantastic actress putting together her part. She was lover, cook, and wife, and all these facets of Nina, the tenderness of the wife, the seductiveness of the mistress, the square honesty of the cook, all these qualities Dame Edith summoned up for the part at our preliminary dress rehearsal at the Haymarket, before we went up to Liverpool to open. It was a rehearsal the like of which I've never seen, an absolute glory. I thought then that all was well, and we'd got over the worst of the hurdles. Kay watched that rehearsal, hidden at the back of the dress circle, and was absolutely bowled over by the quality of Dame Edith's work.

But when I got to the Adelphi Hotel in Liverpool on the Sunday before the dress rehearsal, Hugh Beaumont told me that Dame Edith had had a breakdown. The doctor was with her and didn't know if she would even be able to play the opening night, let alone the dress rehearsal next day. I was shattered and said how sorry I was, but when I asked if there was any chance of my seeing her later, he said that would be absolutely fatal. The responsibility for her indisposition was clearly mine.

The dress rehearsal was upon us. The understudy whom the management had engaged had failed to learn Dame Edith's lines, so we were reduced to having her read the part. It was a ghastly occasion, and left us all despondent, hoping and praying that Dame Edith would recover in time to play the opening night. But it wasn't to be. I had no one to blame but myself. My inexperience as a director, my six-day-week commitment to *Bell, Book and Candle* conspired with the preoccupations of my own life to produce a failure on my part which still makes me shudder.

Roussin, the author, arrived from Paris hoping to see a great performance from Dame Edith and found the understudy reading the part. The play was very much Nina's play, and David Hutcheson and James Hayter, excellent actors as they are, were quite unable to hold it up. It was a total shambles. I'd been given the night off from *Bell, Book and Candle,* and I stood at the back of the circle listening to the understudy, realizing what a mistake I'd made with the set, and watching the audience slowly abandoning the theatre. I went and found a drink in a pub opposite the theatre and stood there at the bar, dazed and miserable, until it was time to seek out André Roussin and apologize to him.

I went back to London to resume my part in *Bell, Book and Candle* and to discuss with Hugh Beaumont what must be done with *Nina,* and who could be put in at such short notice. We decided to bring in Michael Hordern, in lieu of David Hutcheson, for the part of the lover. Then we sent for Coral Browne, who very quickly learned the part of Nina Tessier, and who subsequently played it in London as well as in the provinces.

Coral Browne, Hayter, and Hordern opened at the Haymarket in July, 1955; but the play obviously didn't work and we had a large flop. I was sorry for Binkie Beaumont, who'd behaved wonderfully throughout, giving me all the succor he could, but it had been an impossible task.

Meanwhile, *Bell, Book and Candle* was also having a strange career. After a few months Lilli left the play, and here again I had to replace my leading lady. For this part the management chose Joan Greenwood, and she was brilliant and unique—I loved working with her. Then eventually I myself was allowed out, to go to America for *My Fair Lady,* on condition that H. M. Tennent had first refusal to do the musical in London and was given a small percentage of the profits in New York. Not a bad deal, this time, for Hugh Beaumont.

Oddly enough, when Joan Greenwood in her turn left the Van Druten play, Hugh Beaumont engaged Kay to tour in the lead. So while I was rehearsing and playing a pretour of *My Fair Lady,* Kay took over in *Bell, Book and Candle,* which in certain quarters came to be known as *Bell, Book and Kendall.* When her tour finished she joined me in New York, where *My Fair Lady* had just had its successful opening. What joy to have her with me, after the long weeks apart! I could hardly believe it was happening—here I was with a terrific success on my hands and with my love. How could anybody be so lucky?

When Kay joined me in New York just after the opening of *My Fair Lady,* we had the good fortune to find a charming house on Long Island, near Westbury, belonging to Michael Phipps, the polo player, who was then in Palm Beach, and all seemed set fair. The house was fun, and we persuaded our great friends Dirk Bogarde and Tony Forward to come out from London for a visit. Lifelong friends of Kay's, they had often had us to stay in England.

The summer of 1956 was a lovely, mad time. Kay used to play all sorts of practical jokes and loved to cause a disturbance whenever she could, simply for fun. She would, for instance, quietly disappear in the middle of an evening. I would go upstairs to see what had happened to her, and then ask if anyone else had seen her. Then we would go out into the garden and institute a search there. Finally we would get really worried and set off in cars, driving down the lanes and through the woods, and come back again empty-handed. Kay, meanwhile, had been watching these goings-on from some hiding place behind a tree or an outbuilding, and having caused all this uproar, would make a tremendous entrance from the garden, with her face covered with soil, and pretend she had had the most awful time of it, and be delighted with the fuss she had occasioned.

Toward the autumn she started to complain of headaches and general lassitude. I was tired as well after nearly a year's run, and we both went into the Harkness Pavilion in New York for checkups. A few weeks later Dr. Atchley, the head diagnostician, a much-admired doctor, called and said he would like to see Kay again for some extra blood tests, and she went along. Nothing more happened, for a little time, until Atchley telephoned me at the theatre and asked me to go and see him.

Kay was leaving to make a film in Hollywood after Christmas, *Les Girls* with George Cukor, and some foreboding kept me from going to see Dr. Atchley until she was on her way. It was our first and last carefree Christmas together. She was in very good spirits when I saw her off, knowing that I would be going out to spend two weeks with her shortly when I had a break from the show. After she left I telephoned Atchley and made an appointment to go to see him at the Harkness Pavilion on Wednesday, January 2, 1957, between the matinee and the evening performances.

It was a grim meeting. Dr. Atchley hummed and hawed, and said he realized Kay and I were not married, and that I was still married to another woman, but that he did not know any of Kay's family, and so had had a long deliberation with himself as to what to do—had deliberated, in fact, for many weeks. He seemed old and frail and suddenly indecisive as he told me this. I said, "Please tell me what is the matter with Kay," whereupon he hummed some more, and said I must realize that if he told me, and I accepted the responsibility, it would be at least one jewel in my crown. . . .

I reassured the dedicated and priestlike old man that I wanted to accept responsibility for Kay, whom I loved very much. So he told me then that she had an incurable disease— myeloid leukemia—and had a life expectancy of about two years. I sat, my own blood draining, unable to say anything. A whole vista of agony stretched out before me, and yet I felt proud that this doctor had given me the task of looking after her.

I started to question him about the disease—what happened, what signs were there, what could be done to help?

He said, "There is nothing to be done."

Subsequent research proved this to be untrue. There are now, as I was later to learn, quite a number of things that can be done to alleviate the agony, though not to deflect the inevitable end. To be told that nobody must know, least of all Kay (and she never did know), and at the same time that there was nothing I could do, gave me a feeling of overwhelming loneliness.

I went back to the theatre to do the evening show. It was

very hard. The doctor's words, "There is nothing you can do," kept pounding through my head. If only I had known more about the disease—but he had told me nothing. He had not even told me about the basic structure of the red and white corpuscles, and how the body's resistance to any kind of disease would gradually deteriorate. He had not told me what "myeloid" meant, and I had to discover for myself that it referred to the bone marrow, and that this form of the disease also infected the glands.

I kept wondering how I was going to manage the years to come, how I was going to get divorced from Lilli, whether I could keep up the pretense of hope without ever letting Kay realize the deception. Poor Katie, working so hard in Hollywood, oblivious.

It was clear to me what I ought to do and wanted to do. I must take care of her. I must be constantly by her side. I would marry her, because I loved her.

I was totally given to this new task, and it was my joy. The next two years were without doubt the worst and yet the best years of my life.

I went on with the show until my holiday came, then joined Kay in Hollywood. She was full of life and very gay and loving. We shared a house in Beverly Hills with Terence Rattigan and Gladys Cooper's corgi, called June. I went along with Atchley's prescription, "There is nothing to be done"—and for a few months there was not. I confided in no one, I did not dare to, for fear that that person by look or deed would give something away to Kay.

She finished *Les Girls* in fine shape. I went back to New York to continue with *My Fair Lady,* and she followed me. While we were living in the Phippses' house we had made friends with Jock Whitney and his wife. They had a boathouse in Port Washington, on the Sound, a large and very beautiful building; the skipper of the Whitney yacht lived in one side of the quarters, and Jock now let us have the other side, which we fixed up a little. I bought a Chris-Craft speedboat and, living right on the Sound, we were able to take it out almost every day. Before I went in to work, we bathed, or, if Kay was not up to going out—she had started to have headaches again quite badly—I would go out fishing for flounder. On weekends we would take the boat a long way up the Sound, beyond Oyster Bay, which was then very beautiful and unspoiled.

By June, 1957, Kay was beginning to show grave signs of her illness, and I consulted another doctor, recommended by Dr. Atchley. The problem was to get blood tests taken regularly without alarming Kay, and I used the pretext that her anemia needed constant checking. She had been anemic all her life, which made the pretext sound more likely. I was told that the rogue cells had quietened down, and that there was as yet no need for blood transfusions or any other medication. This sounded a little more hopeful: at least there was something that could be done, when the time came. The new doctor said Kay might easily go on as she was for a year at least, with occasional bad headaches and fatigue, and this proved to be the case. She had such an incredible amount of go and *joie de vivre* in her, it was impossible to believe it could ever die.

The only other soul I had had to confide in was my friend and lawyer, Aaron Frosch, who helped me to get a Mexican divorce and to plan my remarriage. Kay and I were married on June 23, 1957, by the Reverend Dr. Charles Potter, in a strange little church in New York, the Universalist Church of the Divine Paternity. It was kept open after the show, and we were married after midnight, attended only by Kay's sister, Kim, and my witness, Aaron Frosch. Kay was terribly nervous and spent the time either giggling quietly or having little weeps. I held onto her and occasionally gave her small punches to try to stop her, because I was afraid she might upset Dr. Potter.

I had put the ring on her finger, but I felt that Kay had not found the ceremony properly satisfying, so we had a second service about a week later, in the garden of my old friend

Leland Hayward, with a delightful justice of the peace and a photographer and lots of guests. Next door lived Bill Paley, head of CBS, and his wife, Babe, and they and the Jock Whitneys also brought friends. It was a lovely day, and this time Kay was very solemn and enjoyed it very much. So indeed did I.

Throughout the run of *My Fair Lady* Kay always came into New York with me, but it was quite a strain keeping her entertained. Matinee days were especially tiresome. It was a long stretch for Kay, with nothing to do in the afternoons or evenings. She had seen most of the films and was much too highly strung to sit and read a book. She wasn't very good at entertaining herself, so she would go off to Sardi's and chat with people, have a few drinks and something to eat, and pick me up after the show, rather the worse for wear but always very jolly. We would then have supper in town before being driven back to the boathouse. Otherwise Kay rested a lot, and if sometimes she did not feel well enough to go out, she put it down to her damned anemia—thank God.

Summer turned to autumn and soon my second year in *My Fair Lady* was over, and we were able to go back to Portofino. I remember Kay looking through one of those terrible Italian magazines, as we drove along the coast toward Portofino, and picking out one word of the Italian in an article about her. She said, "Look at this rubbish, they seem to be saying I've got leukemia."

"Obviously," I said, "they mean anemia."

Kay seemed satisfied—but what can you say for those scandal magazines? It is hard to imagine the callousness of a mind which will release such information without considering the harm it may do.

We took a house in St. Moritz for a winter holiday, and it was there that Kay became so ill she could not get out of bed. I called in Dr. Berry, whom I knew, and told him the truth, pledging him to secrecy, and we moved her to the clinic. Here I had luck. A professor in Zürich had invented a pill to retard the action of the cancer cells, and he came to St. Moritz. His treatment prolonged Kay's life by at least a year, for she reacted very well to the pills; after three weeks her blood became almost normal. And now that she was in the hospital —the first time she had been bad enough to go to the hospital without being too alarmed—it was also easier to have her blood checked and to give her blood transfusions. It seemed after all that "nothing to be done" was an unnecessarily pessimistic prognosis.

I roamed around the town of St. Moritz, lost. I used to go and watch the Cresta Run teams practicing sometimes, but I did not like to be away from her too long and soon found my way back to the clinic. I felt a little less apprehensive since finding the professor, and my whole mission in life was to keep Kay's spirits up, and at all costs not to let her know the truth.

We were due to do a film together in Paris for Metro-Goldwyn-Mayer, called *The Reluctant Debutante,* based on a play by William Douglas-Home, with Vincente Minnelli directing. I did not put MGM off, I kept them in suspense: Kay was very much looking forward to the picture and I wanted her to do all the work she could, to take her mind off her illness.

While Kay was convalescing we had Terry Rattigan to stay, with a friend, and both my sons, Noel and Carey, and my niece, Miranda Fyfe. Kay made a remarkable recovery, and then we thought it would be good to get out of the house where she had been so ill, so we went to Klosters, where we had been before and enjoyed ourselves.

No one and nothing could keep Katie down. She had the courage of a lion. Soon we were doing a little mild tobogganing—and Katie fell off into the snow and cracked a bone in her pelvis. We went to Zürich, on our way to Paris for *The Reluctant Debutante,* and had X rays taken; fortunately it was only a splinter, not too serious. While we were there we visited our professor and had a good report.

With Kay in *The Reluctant Debutante* (Metro-Goldwyn-Mayer)

We told the film company nothing of Kay's illness or the accident to her pelvis. Katie did all the preproduction interviews lying on a chaise longue, looking very glamorous, but never on her feet before either producer or director. They did not suspect that she could not stand, and by the time the film was ready to shoot the bone had mended. Admittedly we had had to do some double talk, altering the script and then asking William Douglas-Home over to rewrite much of the play which, rewritten in Hollywood terms, had lost some of its sparkle.

Katie weathered the film well. The Swiss pills were still working; every few weeks a test had to be made, and the number of pills adjusted, one, two, or three a day. Then, when the blood count came up to normal again, they could be stopped for a time.

We went to London for my year at Drury Lane in *My Fair Lady,* with rehearsals starting April 7, 1958. We took the Earl of Warwick's house—it was on his yacht that we had spent that black afternoon with Lilli, in Portofino so long ago. Kay used to come to Drury Lane with me and sit in my elegant dressing room with her two pugs, Woolsack and Higgins, who'd been given us by Dirk Bogarde and Tony Forward during the American run of *My Fair Lady.*

It was good to be near Kay's London doctor, Dr. Goldman. He was very fond of her—he had driven over snowbound and icy roads to see her in St. Moritz—and a tower of strength to me.

During the London run her health got worse, as the Swiss pills lost most of their effectiveness. Sometimes I would come back to the house in Cheyne Walk after the show to find her having a blood transfusion in the bedroom. I remember I got a week off from the show and we were planning to go down to Ste. Maxime to stay with Prince Bertil of Sweden, when one night just before we were to leave, Kay had a very bad transfusion. Perhaps her system was beginning to refuse any new blood, which, I had been told, is what eventually happens.

151

She ran a raging temperature, about 105 degrees, with frightful rigors, and Goldman and I stayed with her putting cold compresses on her legs to get the fever down. The next day she was on the train for the South of France, and then she was dancing all over Bertil's house. I could not believe it, but it always happened. She defied death with her spirit.

Despite her illness she wanted to do a play she had found while I was at Drury Lane, so I directed it and got the Winter Garden Theatre for her, and arranged for Gladys Cooper to act in it with her. It was *The Bright One* by Judy Campbell, a charming little play about a schoolmistress on a tour of the Greek islands, who gets lost and changes places with a sprite of magical charms. It did not quite work, but Kay did some fantastic things in it and I tried to keep it running at a loss for her sake, until, quite rightly, my more commercially-minded partner insisted that we take it off. During the run Kay's health kept up and she did not miss a single performance.

My year at Drury Lane ended in April, 1959, and Kay was entering the last phase of her illness. Metro, though, had made an offer for her to play in a film in Paris written by a friend, Harry Kurnitz, called *Once More With Feeling*, with Yul Brynner as the leading man. I had a long session with Dr. Goldman, and after much debate we jointly decided it would be better for her to do it. We could not admit defeat because we both knew that she would never do so.

So I accompanied her to Paris and we fought our way through this last film. She contracted pneumonia and had a terrible infection in her intestines—the smallest infection would almost immediately turn into something grave, because she was virtually devoid of those corpuscles essential to fight disease. She struggled on. There were the usual long and tiring hours in front of the cameras, and then radiation treatment at the American Hospital in Paris, and blood transfusions, before going back again the next day to the studios. On it went, day after day, as the film painfully took shape. There was a doctor in Paris who helped me secretly, and our old friend Dr. Goldman was close at hand. For me the hours were endless while Kay was working, but I could not haunt the studios all the time and perhaps let her suspect my gnawing concern. I tried to while away the time by playing golf at St. Cloud, which was near the studios, in the company of Sydney Chaplin, whom Kate had known and liked for years. My golf was atrocious, but Sydney never complained.

The film limped on. Every time Kate was too ill to go to work they tried to shoot around her. The production was in trouble with the insurance company for taking her on, but still we kept the truth from them. I could never let her be examined by an outside doctor, because even a cursory examination would show the terrible enlargement of her spleen.

She finished the film, brave, wonderful soul, and we got on the train to go to Portofino: the last stage for her. In Italy too I had my own doctor, called Gallupo, who was also in the know. Kay had only been back a week, in bed, when Gallupo said he would like her in his clinic at Rapallo so that he could get a professor from Genoa to see if there was something that could be done.

I went with poor darling Kay to Rapallo and there were no vacant visitors' rooms so I had to go back to the villa every night and sleep fitfully, thinking of my beloved with rigors and pains that were fit to kill a giant—but not her. Finally I could not stand it. It were almost better that she died at the villa, except that no aids could have been given for her comfort, and no blood. I called Goldman. He came down to Rapallo and moved her at once back to the villa, and next day she made her last journey back to London by train to enter the London Clinic. Even then, the photographers would not leave her alone; they followed her to the doors of the London Clinic, and she turned on them and said, "Don't think I'm coming here to die. I'm not." She died a week later.

I was given a room next to hers at the clinic and was with her all that week. Toward the end she was under heavy sedation, and after all the pain she had borne so gallantly she mercifully lapsed into a deep coma and was at peace when she died.

Before I left the London Clinic that day, I held Dr. Goldman in my arms and thanked him for his help. For over two years I had known that her days were numbered. Perhaps she did too? After all, all our days are numbered. But I kept my promise, I kept the secret, and I'm glad I did. We had a better time that way, even if she suspected. There was always the glimmer of hope: perhaps a cure . . . ? perhaps a miracle?

The rest of the day went by and I found myself in the peaceful gloom of a West End church—and then another, and yet another. I sat in a pew near the back, just sitting, not consciously praying, dumbly trying to accept and understand that Kay's vital spark had gone out forever.

At that moment my philosophy of tomorrow left me. For me, there were no tomorrows, there was only yesterday.

CHAPTER EIGHT

My Fair Lady

I<small>T</small> was in the summer of 1955, while I was in the middle of the London run of *Bell, Book and Candle,* that three gentlemen came to see me about a musical with the tentative title of *Lady Liza.* They were Alan Jay Lerner, the dramatic author and lyricist who had written *Brigadoon* and *Paint Your Wagon,* Fritz Loewe, the composer, and the lawyer Herman Levin, who had produced a number of plays on Broadway. Among them they had acquired the rights to Bernard Shaw's *Pygmalion,* and they proposed to turn it into a musical—*the* musical, *My Fair Lady.*

They played me the music of the preliminary version, which included several numbers that were later dropped from the production, and I'm sure Alan and Fritz will forgive me if I say that the music they then had was not up to the standard of the final version. There was a number called "Lady Liza," a very pushy sort of Broadway tune which Fritz later turned into a waltz and used in the ballroom scene, and another for Higgins called "Please Don't Marry Me," which I didn't care for at all and they didn't like very much either. The only number that really whizzed along, when they first

arrived, was "The Rain in Spain"—that was about all they
had in the way of show tunes, and it was obviously a great
one. But they hadn't written "Why Can't the English Learn
to Speak?," they hadn't written "I've Grown Accustomed to
Her Face," and they hadn't written "Why Can't a Woman
Be More Like a Man?"

At that time there had been only one musical made from a
Shaw play, and that had annoyed Shaw tremendously; it was
called *The Chocolate Soldier* and had been taken, without
permission, from *Arms and the Man*. Now Alan and Fritz and
Herman Levin were all anxious for me to play Professor
Henry Higgins, but I was doubtful about it, especially because
I had never sung. And yet it was a marvelous part, and I
knew it quite well, having seen it played a couple of times,
by Raymond Massey and by John Clements. It occurred to
me early on that if I could get a guarantee that the key scenes
in *Pygmalion* would be included in the musical, I would have
some security, but even so it was quite a step to take, and I
could not make up my mind. Of the people in London whose
advice I sought, several said it would be a terrible thing for
me to do, and Sir Malcolm Sargent called the musical a dis-
graceful notion.

In my usual way, I vacillated, while continuing to see Levin
and Loewe and Lerner. We went for long walks in the park
together, and I found that Alan Lerner had a very good mind
and was certainly a great devotee of Shaw. I knew also that
Fritz Loewe was a brilliant composer. From time to time, too,
we gathered around the piano and sang passages from Gilbert
and Sullivan together. Loewe and Lerner wanted to find out
my vocal range: they told me later it was one and a half notes.

After three weeks I decided to chance it. I very nearly
didn't do it, I must say, and my final decision was, in large
part, based on my private life. I felt that it might be a very
good thing to put some distance between myself and my problems, not only so as to take a long look at my marriage to
Lilli, but also to see how really deep my feelings were for

Katie. I thought maybe time away would settle something, and indeed it did.

Alan and Fritz went off to America while I went on playing *Bell, Book and Candle*. I had about six months in which to prepare for *My Fair Lady,* and I thought I had better start by having my voice trained in some way. I took counsel, and went in the first instance to a maestro in Wigmore Street who taught bel canto. He was very dominating and forceful, and it took me only three visits to realize beyond all doubt that I would never be a singer, not in the accepted sense of the word. Alan and Fritz would be returning in a few months with all the new material that they were writing, and although the contracts were agreed I still wanted to do myself a little justice, even at this early stage. I telephoned Alan in America, and after I'd explained my problems with bel canto singing, he referred me to a man called Bill Low, who conducted the orchestra in the pit at the Coliseum.

Bill Low was very much more helpful; he'd been closely connected with musical comedies and as a conductor had realized all kinds of techniques of singing, and so we started to work together. I had a piano moved into my hotel suite— I was only allowed to play it at certain hours of the day—and we went over the numbers Alan and Fritz had brought originally. To begin with Low really looked glum, but then a very interesting thing happened. He told me not to think about singing the words but to start by just saying them. He said, "There is such a thing as talking on pitch—using only those notes that you want to use, picking them out of the score, sometimes more, sometimes less. For the rest of the time, concentrate on staying on pitch, even though you're only speaking." This advice came as a revelation to me, and I practiced away, with Bill's constant encouragement and help, and thus created the style which I used in *My Fair Lady*. I think I was the first actor to use it as a singing style, and it wouldn't have worked without my having an innate sense of rhythm.

On their next visit to London, Alan Lerner and Fritz Loewe brought a number called "I'm an Ordinary Man," to replace "Please Don't Marry Me," and the opening number, "Why Can't the English . . . ?" We still had "The Rain in Spain," and they'd been building up Eliza's numbers as well. "Ordinary Man" I loved on first hearing. It was a brilliant, long, and complicated number, but with a very easy soft-shoe rhythm, with a lilt to it and an easy delivery, and I enjoyed it very much. "Why Can't the English . . . ?" I worried about. I said to Alan that it sounded far too much like Noël Coward, too reminiscent of "Mad Dogs and Englishmen"; it needed breaking down and changing, it had a too familiar tang. Well, that song was worked on and worked on. Right through rehearsal Fritz was still playing with it so that I shouldn't come on as Henry Higgins and sound like Noël Coward, and in the event I think he succeeded.

Off they went again to carry on the good work, while I went on practicing with Bill Low. I didn't want to embark on "Why Can't the English . . . ?" as yet, and "The Rain in Spain" was really a trio, so I didn't bother much with it; but "Ordinary Man" I did with Bill Low, and got fairly straight.

When I arrived in New York at Christmas, 1955, Alan and Fritz had just finished "Accustomed to Her Face." They told me they'd got the last number for Higgins, and I went over to Alan's house, where as usual they played it for me. They knew I couldn't read a note of music, so Fritz played and Alan sang—a very nice singing voice Alan has, much better than mine. I realized the beauty of the melody, as well as its simplicity. It was an acting tour de force, with musical accompaniment, and I was thrilled—I just hoped I could do justice to this marvelous piece of work.

After they'd sung a number over for me, I used to take the lyric and, with Fritz playing the piano, or sometimes with somebody who sat in for Fritz and knew exactly what Fritz's phrases were, I'd start working it, right off the bat, mapping it out, and finding the right pitch. "Accustomed to Her Face" was written right in my range, which by then I suppose extended to three notes, and I fiddled around with it for quite a bit before the rehearsals, so that by the time I got to rehearsal it only took polishing.

To play the part of Pickering they chose Bob Coote, who had been a close friend of mine for years. He was the perfect choice, and nobody has ever been better in the role. He had a spot in the second act, a very entertaining comedy turn with a telephone call, more in the manner of P. G. Wodehouse than of George Bernard Shaw, talking to a friend in the Foreign Office called Boozie. After the first reading, with Alan Lerner singing all the numbers and Fritz playing the piano to the assembled cast, Alan and Fritz and I got together with Moss Hart, the director, and Fritz pointed out that Higgins has no musical material between his entrance after the ball and "Accustomed to Her Face." We all agreed that this made for an imbalance in the show, and we decided the only place to put another musical number for Higgins was at the point where Eliza has gone back to Covent Garden, to her native heath, and Higgins learns of her departure, and to intersperse the number with Pickering's telephone call.

I went back with Alan to the Hotel Pierre, where we discussed the wording of the number. It was Nancy Olson, his then wife, who came up with an idea for the title, a brilliant idea conceived more in anger than in jest. Alan like many of us enjoyed the company of men and liked to go out in the evening drinking and chatting. This had evidently irked Nancy, and she said, "Why don't you call it 'Why Can't a Woman Be More Like a Man?'" Lyrics writers frequently need to find a title before they can get the lyrics going, and of course this was an inspiration; though Alan had quite a few problems with the lyrics even after that, and the song didn't reach me until almost the last week of rehearsals, just before we opened in New Haven.

When this new material was added it meant that Pickering's telephone call is interrupted by Higgins coming onstage and disappearing and coming back again some three or four times while he is dressing, until with the last stanza he leaves the house to try to find Eliza. There was a great deal of the telephone call left, but it was less of a tour de force, and I think Bob found it hard to forgive, as anyone might have, the way we had broken into a good moment. For a long time our old friendship was strained, though I am happy to say we are now friends again.

We were very fortunate in having Moss Hart to direct the play. He was one of the great figures of the American theatre. He knew the business inside out, not only from the direction and production angle, but also as a writer. He collaborated with the formidable George S. Kaufman on such plays as *You Can't Take It with You* and *The Man Who Came to Dinner,* and also wrote *Lady in the Dark,* in which Gertrude Lawrence appeared. He was a really delightful man, an enthusiastic fan of the theatre, and he genuinely admired actors and encouraged them in their work with enormous patience.

My Fair Lady was of course a big and unwieldy show to get together, and Moss Hart had the chorus rehearsing in one theatre and the principals at another—at the famous New Amsterdam, where the *Ziegfeld Follies* had played in the Thirties. By the Fifties the entrance to the New Amsterdam was downright squalid; we worked cheek by jowl with the blue movies and the striptease shows. We made our way through a crowd of strange-looking characters lounging about, to take the elevator up to the third floor to what had been a very glamorous theatre in Ziegfeld's day, a theatre now falling down and smelling of decay.

Moss Hart had things so organized that after ten days he was able to have a run-through of the play; this meant roughly doing all the numbers, and all that was left of Shaw's play—which was quite a lot—roughly but in the proper sequence. I was still holding the book, naturally, and reading the part, and so were Julie Andrews and the chorus, but crude

160

as it was a run-through at this stage was a miracle of organization.

Julie Andrews was not as yet a great star, and her knowledge of serious theatre was limited. She had done *The Boy Friend* and was known as a singer, as little Julie Andrews, a young girl with a fantastic voice. At first she was bemused by my interpretation of Higgins, and even giggled in my face when I became completely involved in the role. Thankfully she got over that, and in the three years we played together we never had a cross word of any kind.

For the part of Eliza Julie had to acquire a Cockney accent. Her instructor in Cockney was an American: through long familiarity with American films British audiences have become attuned to the Brooklyn or Chicago accent, but a Broadway audience would have had difficulty in understanding an undiluted Cockney twang.

For Stanley Holloway, a master of dialect, no such problem arose. His experience, strength, and humor particularly in his musical numbers contributed an incalculable amount to the success of the show. He repeated his virtuoso performance with equal success in the film. In spite of what Stanley and I still regard as a mischief-making newspaper report, our relations through the New York and London runs were excellent and still are. For the record, we have both forgiven the man who wrote it.

I had as my mother in the New York production Cathleen Nesbitt, that wonderful actress who was the great love of Rupert Brooke's short life. She is still extremely active, and when she comes to dinner with us in London she still takes the stairs at a brisk trot at the age of eighty-five.

I was very lucky with mothers, because Zena Dare, the great pinup girl of the Nineties, played the part in London; and the incomparable Gladys Cooper, in the film. I felt that Henry Higgins was fairly secure although no father Higgins was ever referred to—perhaps because Shaw personally would have preferred an immaculate conception to any other.

When we began to rehearse the numbers, in the evenings, I did them as I'd planned, with a piano on the stage and with the arranger and the conductor sitting in the audience. They were almost as concerned as I was about Professor Higgins' singing abilities. The conductor was a dear man called Franz Allers, who bore with me for two whole years. I could not use him in the way a singer does: I never waited for his beat, he had to catch mine; I never looked at him, he had to follow me. This was quite revolutionary. I would start a number straight out of dialogue and go into the song, without changing tempo, and this was something that he'd never had to cope with, and created a problem for him in bringing the orchestra in at the exact moment. But he always managed to do it, and although my rhythm patterns were never quite the same from night to night we always caught up with each other fore or aft. He was the most generous man, and never failed to come backstage to my dressing room after each performance.

During rehearsals Julie used to encourage me by saying, "Just wait until you get the orchestra, it's like a marvelous sort of eiderdown, you can relax into it." That of course is true if you are a singer. But with nonsingers it is not quite the same thing. There is an extraordinary difference between standing by a piano where only the melody is being played, and having an orchestra where you can't even hear the melody, because they're playing around the melody. There had to be a melodic theme in the orchestra for me to follow, and this was arranged. But when, after six weeks of frantic rehearsals, we went up to New Haven for a preview on the Saturday night, with the real opening on Monday, I had only had one rehearsal with the orchestra in a room. I did a couple of run-throughs with them on the New Haven stage but was far too frightened to get even near a melody by this time. The whole idea of having this vast orchestra playing away while I was doing my song-talk really was petrifying . . . I don't think I've ever been as frightened before or since in my life. At the last moment I begged them to call off the Saturday-evening benefit and wait for the official opening on the Monday. There was such a furor, however, and so many people waiting outside the theatre, in spite of the atrocious wet weather and the flurries of snow, that eventually I was persuaded to grit my teeth and try to get through it. And though I would have been lost without Franz Allers and his orchestra I still had to ignore them. This was still the case two years later and one hot summer's day Franz came in to conduct the matinee in a white coat, and I had to send a message down saying, "Please, please take off that coat, I can see you." I still had to pretend the orchestra wasn't there.

It was a very long show when we opened. I think we rang the curtain up about eight-thirty and we were down about twelve-forty-five, an exhausting evening for actors and audience. We had a ballet in it, which was never seen again, a scene in which Higgins groomed Eliza for the ball, which really centered on the chorus dressing her up while she sang a tune called "Shy"; and I also had a number called "Come to the Ball," which I performed only that once, because of the length of the show. There was a lot of regrouping up in New Haven, but the show seemed, despite its length, to be going well, and Fritz held a champagne soiree up in the dress circle with the girls from the chorus.

We then went off to Philadelphia, where we played for four weeks with such success that people began to talk about a smash hit, and "wowing them in New York." This worried me, and I said, "For God's sake don't go on talking as if it were already an enormous hit. We haven't done it yet." During the Philadelphia stay we rehearsed every day, as well as performing at night, and knocked the play into shape, cutting little bits here and little bits there. And so to the opening in New York, where of course *My Fair Lady* was a smash hit, as the optimists had predicted.

My contract for *My Fair Lady* was for nine months only— but how could you leave a show like that? It was all far too exciting, and I stayed with it for two years, and finally another year at Drury Lane. A considerable part of one's life, three years, and when you come to think of it, a long, long run, for an actor, is rather like a lawyer having to plead the same case, year in and year out, or a housewife having to cook the same meal every night, and eat it too.

During the run both Julie and I took little breaks—we had about a week off a year, and occasionally also we lost our voices, so that understudies had to take over. The first time this happened to me was very early on in the run; we opened on Thursday, and cut the *My Fair Lady* record the following Sunday, and what with one thing and another I was left speechless. I took a few days off and went to Bermuda with Kay to recover, to try to get back voice and strength; whereupon my understudy lost his voice, and during the very first number. He was totally inaudible, and the management had to do something very rarely done: they closed the show with the performance incomplete and gave the public its money back. They called me up in Bermuda in desperation, but from my husky whispering realized I could not possibly do the show, so then they managed to find another actor, a second understudy. One way or another I had several understudies in this part, and an awful lot of people played Higgins over the years, after I had left the show.

Throughout the New York run of *My Fair Lady* in the Fifties there was a sustained atmosphere of exhilaration. Even before the curtain went up there was a great sense of expectancy out front, that buzz of tense excitement that fills the air with electricity. And after the show we came out of the stage door to find there an immense queue camping out all night, summer and winter, with Thermos flasks and rugs, waiting for the box office to open so that they could buy standing room for the next evening's show.

The general *esprit* of the company was extraordinary too. The "kids," as we called them, the chorus, used to crowd into the wings to watch the numbers, and it was really like belonging to a team of experts. I don't think I once did "Accustomed to Her Face" without an audience backstage as well as in front. We all had the same feeling that we were taking part in something out of the ordinary, and that it might be the only time in our lives that we would be connected with anything quite like it.

My cramped dressing room at the theatre was the scene of some memorable occasions—Marilyn Monroe doing wondrous things while looking at herself in two mirrors simultaneously; Spencer Tracy coming in with Frank Sinatra and saying rather sweetly, "You made the little wop cry!"; Louis Armstrong looking at me and in *that* voice saying, "You hit every note right down the middle, man"; Charles Laughton asking if he could watch it again from the side of the stage. To me these were giant compliments from giants. Cole Porter reserved himself a seat once a week for the entire run. Perhaps the biggest moment for me professionally was the Actors' Benefit performance when a special Sunday show was given in aid of theatrical charities so that all actors and actresses could see it.

I have—just once—managed to see *My Fair Lady* from the audience. Kay and I had been away for my annual break in Jamaica, where Noël Coward had lent us his house, and when we got back we thought we'd rather like to go and see the show. There wasn't a seat, of course, vacant, but they gave us a couple of chairs, at the very back of the theatre, and we sat there and watched, unknown to anybody. Edward Mulhare was playing my part, as he played it for a long time after I left the show. I thought he was very good, and I was enchanted with the whole performance. The play looked like a jewel— I couldn't believe it. Although I'd been playing in it all that time, I'd had no idea how perfect and beautiful it looked.

Some strange things happened in the course of the run. There was one period when a mad bomber was going around New York planting bombs in odd places, and he apparently had sent a letter to the Mark Hellinger Theatre one evening, saying he had put a bomb somewhere near the front row, timed to go off while I was doing "Accustomed to Her Face." When I made my exit from one side of the stage and was going around the back of the stage to go on for this number, the stage manager said, "Don't worry, Rex, if it's a bit noisy."

I thought, That's very funny—I wonder what he means, a bit noisy? I went on and of course the bomb did not go off. Later I went back to Biff Liff, the stage manager, and asked what he meant about things being noisy, and he told me about the bomb scare. He said he had had to take the gamble, he couldn't tell me not to go on. I stared, and finally said, "Well, it appears that I am expendable."

"Accustomed to Her Face" seemed to be a dangerous number. On another occasion I was halfway through the song when a very heavy set which had been "flown"—hoisted above the stage—fell immediately behind the frontcloth where I was performing. There was a thunderous crash, splinters and quite large pieces of wood came flying under the cloth, which had billowed out almost knocking me into the orchestra pit.

When I recovered from the shock, a matter of a few seconds, I found the stage littered and in total silence. The orchestra had stopped. Franz Allers had had such a fright that he obviously had forgotten to keep his arms whirling about. I had a moment of desperation, then, I suppose because I was hell-bent doing the number to a full house, recovered quicker than Allers (at whom I still didn't dare to look), and called loudly for a clarinet—mostly because it was about the only instrument in the orchestra I could think of—but I needed an introductory chord to get me back into action. There was a pause, then up came rather shakily from the pit the notes I needed and I finished the number to tumultuous applause.

When I came off I didn't know what I would find; it was a shambles, but incredibly nobody was hurt. We had been running nearly two years by then and apparently the ropes that supported this heavy set had frayed. It was a ghastly thought that had it fallen three or four minutes later we would have been taking our curtain calls and a great number of us would have been very badly injured if not killed.

Finally, the two years came to an end. The last night was a very moving experience. During the party onstage afterward the kids gave me a key ring with a medallion which had my initials on one side and on the other the address in Wimpole Street where Higgins' house was situated. I was saddened at saying good-bye to the "family"—they were a great company.

In London we opened at the Drury Lane, a theatre steeped in tradition, surrounded by streets—Garrick Street, Kemble Street, Betterton Street, Stukeley Street, Macklin Street—named after actors who played in London from the Restoration onward. And much of the action of *My Fair Lady* took place in Covent Garden, perhaps fifty yards away from Drury Lane, which gave it an added flavor.

We had a series of very glamorous premieres for the royal family, five or six in all, before we finally opened. The Queen received us on the stage and talked to everybody. With the exception of the chorus, the cast was virtually the same as had battled through two years on Broadway, so that in a sense the show was a foregone conclusion, and foregone conclusions are never as exciting as the original thing. The year passed uneventfully, compared to the New York run; my preoccupation with Kay's illness, which was growing more acute, outweighed my anxieties about the theatre, though I never ceased getting a thrill out of going on the Drury Lane stage, which is very large and acoustically absolutely brilliant. And Arthur Barbosa did a marvelous job on my dressing room there, making it look as though it belonged to the nineteenth century, with big draperies and chair rails, and some good pieces of furniture which I had hired. Kay spent many hours sitting or lying there, and we received a great many visitors as well. One visit I remember particularly vividly was from Harold Macmillan, who was then Prime Minister. He stayed half an hour and talked brilliantly about the theatre past and present.

The Queen on stage at Drury Lane (Daily Sketch)

He holds the view, as did Churchill, that successful politicians have got to be good actors as well.

Throughout the London run of *My Fair Lady* I was tormented with worry and fear for Kay, which didn't make it easy for me to do the play. I was in fact quite looking forward to the end of the run. I don't think any lay person realizes what a terrible strain it is to do a show so many times. You repeat the dialogue and the lyrics so often that they simply don't make sense anymore, and then if your mind wanders for a second from the words you are saying, you quite suddenly draw a blank. This is a very frightening experience; you pull yourself back, but it gives you such a nervous shock that for the next week you are completely thrown off balance, and have a hard time settling back into a relaxed performance.

I used to carry the lyrics on to the side of the stage and go through them before I went on, which was a torturous thing to have to do, because of course I knew them—I knew them too well. And long parts stay in your subconscious, while you are playing them, for the whole twenty-four hours. That is why it is difficult to do other things; even while you are talking with people, walking, shopping, or reading, the subconscious ticktock goes on. You are geared to just one thing, the performance, and except for that you live in an almost stagnant state. This makes for a strange, disjointed way of life, which other people find hard to bear with, unless they really love and really understand the thing that is called the "acting state."

[CHAPTER NINE]

Beginning Again

A s I look back on the years before and after Kay's death, I see that my judgment and energy were at a low ebb.

Six weeks before Kay died, while she was in Paris making her last film, *Once More with Feeling,* Irene Selznick asked me to go and see a play of Anouilh's, called in French *L'Hurluberlu,* and talked me into doing it for a season in New York, with Peter Brook directing it.

It was not long before a row blew up between Irene Selznick and Peter Brook over the play, and if I had been *compos mentis* I would have understood much more about their differences, and when Irene walked out on the production at the Hotel George V I'd have walked with her. I had a chance to do so; Irene and I had a long talk about it and she said, "There's no reason for you to drop it. Peter wants to go on with it, but he won't go on with it with me." That should have been an eye-opener, because I knew Irene Selznick from the good old days of *Bell, Book and Candle,* and I didn't know Brook.

After Katie died I stayed for a while, very gratefully, with my sister and her husband, who was then Lord Chancellor, living in very dignified surroundings over the Chambers of the House of Lords. During the days I went to Peter Brook's house in Kensington to work on the Anouilh play, which in English was given the title *The Fighting Cock*. Then I moved from Sylvia and David's to stay with Terry Rattigan in Sunningdale, and Peter came down to work with me in the garden.

This was much better. Terry had been a great friend of Kay's and showed himself protective and understanding of my plight. When I said I felt I did not want to go on, he would retort that that was rubbish, that I had to go on—which is the sort of talk one needs from one's friends. Harold French and his wife, Pegs, were also staying at Terry's and did everything they could to be comforting. I spent a lot of time by myself though, thinking over the past. I was awed by Katie's strength of character, was almost happy because of what I had been able to do for her: I had at least made some of her life bearable during those two agonizing years.

When the script of *The Fighting Cock* had at last been translated from the French, and adapted, by Lucienne Hill, we set out for America. My elder sister Marjorie accompanied me, and Michael Gough, who was also in the play. Michael had been at the London Clinic when Katie died and to me he was a guardian in the T. S. Eliot manner.

The Fighting Cock was a satire on De Gaulle. But De Gaulle had been in power for only one year, so that outside France few people recognized the impersonation—particularly as Anouilh had had to soft-pedal the satire to make the French production acceptable to his subject. I played the General, complete with nose, eyebrows, and wig, and strode about my little town in breeches, bossing the villagers and impressing my own clique of friends, and dreamt up all sorts of ridiculous wars and causes.

The joke was not apparent to the Americans—even in England, when the play was performed later at Chichester, it had little success, and in Philadelphia of course the audience simply didn't accept me with noses and character makeup. Little by little I shed my nose, I shed my eyebrows and my

172

wig; eventually I became myself again, which still didn't really help the play, though neither could it have hindered it.

When we got to the ANTA Theatre in New York, *My Fair Lady* was running, ironically, to capacity business two streets away. *The Fighting Cock* played to half-empty houses, and if we found anyone waiting at the stage door it was usually a kind old dear come to say how much she had enjoyed me in *My Fair Lady.* My tomorrows were a long way off—not that success or failure made a damn bit of difference, at that point.

We ran, I think, for ten weeks. I had quite a nice house in Sutton Place, on the East River, where Michael Gough lived with me, and I saw a bit of Larry Olivier, who was directing Charlton Heston in a flop, and was also rather low.

As the play was closing, to my horror an offer came to do a film with Doris Day called *Midnight Lace*—in Hollywood. God, I thought, at this point in my lonely life, what a place to go. But I said yes. I knew I was clutching at straws, but I'd have said yes, I suppose, to anything; it's always easier than saying no, when you don't care.

It was an uncanny experience. I took a house, I had a secretary and two black maids, I had a pool—and I had nothing I liked except a cork tree, which I used to draw. I remember the cork tree well. It must have been hundreds of years old, and I used to sit and make out its shapes.

Doris Day is a dear girl, a kind girl, and a Christian Scientist, as I found out when she lent me some books on the subject. Somehow I managed to lose these, and when at the end of the film she asked for them back, and I had to own up, I felt I was growing horns.

We used to hold what amounted to Christian Science sessions on the set (or so it seemed to me), when all the lights would be put out and the director could be heard telling Doris, *sotto voce,* "God is in the studio, God is in the flowers, God is on the set. . . ." At which point I would wander away and sit down to ponder life and death.

After this bleak episode I retreated to Portofino with guar-

In *Platonov* (John Timbers)

dian friends—Michael Gough, Margaret Leighton, Sybil Row-ley, and my son Noel—and tried to see what could be got out of life, playing it from day to day.

My career looked set to take a dive, and stay in a dive for quite a while, but then George Devine invited me to the Royal Court Theatre, in Sloane Square, to do an early play of Chekhov's called *Platonov*. It is a very long and complex satire on Russian bourgeois society, with an immense cast. I took on the title role and enjoyed it very much, and with Alec Guinness, who was playing in *Ross,* shared the honors in the *Evening Standard* Award for the Best Performance of the Year.

The Royal Court Theatre revived my spirits somewhat. I was very fond of George Devine, who ran the theatre with terrific verve. He was a really big man, in heart and soul, and absolutely honest, a glorious man. Then too it was exciting to play at the Royal Court Theatre, which at that moment was going full blast. It had become known as the writers' theatre, and it gave a first leg up to Osborne, Arden, Wesker, and sundry other Angry Young Men. It was an invigorating place to find myself in suddenly although certainly strange and out of keeping with the rest of my life.

In the cast of *Platonov,* playing Anna Petrovna, was Rachel Roberts, who would later become my wife. Rachel came from Wales, where her father, a dear and humble man, was a Baptist preacher. She had had a lot of misgivings about com-ing to London and to RADA, as she felt very Welsh, quite belligerently Welsh—she expected the English to be a lot of nits and so of course found them to be nits. After working at the Shakespeare Memorial Theatre in Stratford and at the Old Vic, in London and in Bristol, she was now very much at home at the Royal Court Theatre.

She had many friends in the theatrical "angry brigade," and among those who abominated anything that smacked of the establishment. I have never felt that political commitment of any sort contributes to enjoyment in the theatre, and so it

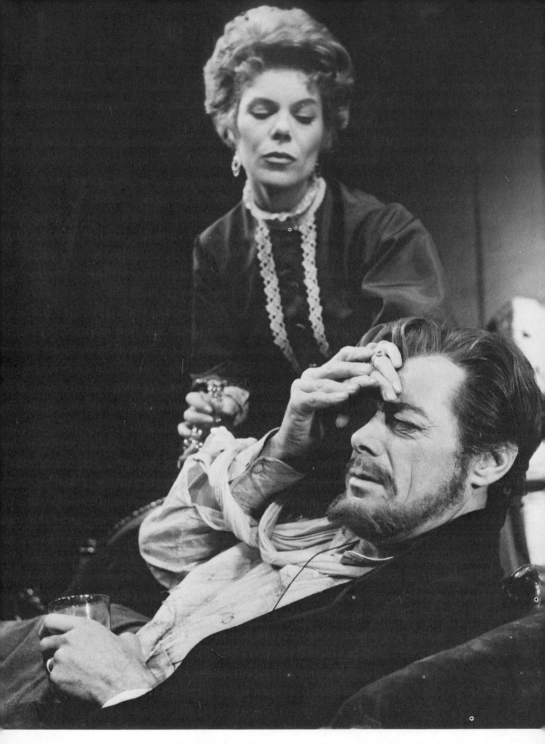
With Rachel Roberts in *Platonov* (John Timbers)

is obvious that Rachel and I had many differences of opinion, and I'm sure that if our minds had been clear we would have seen from the first that we were totally unsuited. Most of the blame, I'm sure, was mine, but I also think that Rachel felt more kindly toward me while I was playing at the Royal Court, her spiritual home, than when I went into big Hollywood films. During the run of *Platonov* we became very fond of each other, and I invited her to come down to Portofino when the play closed.

A further instance of sloppy professional judgment came when I weakly agreed with my agent to go to Madrid to make a film called *The Happy Thieves*, with Rita Hayworth. My agent said something about "getting the money while I could," and instead of sacking him, as I would have done in other years, I fell in with his suggestion. Rita was an old-time friend whom I had got to know when she was married to James Hill. She was desperately shy and uncertain of herself, although she had worked for Columbia for many years and kept that studio going. Rita was absolutely beautiful, the film was absolute rubbish, so bad that the press was asked to stay away and not to review it—as you can imagine, a fairly unusual request. I don't think anyone did see it, luckily.

I returned to the Royal Court with a play by Nigel Dennis called *August for the People,* again with George Devine directing. It had a marvelous first act, an unplayable second act. It opened with a belted earl standing up at a formal dinner and making a speech that started, "Democracy is a dirty word." It was very funny, but people couldn't tell whether it was for or against democracy. It was really Nigel Dennis, who is a great satirist, being Nigel Dennis, but of course the left wing didn't know what to make of this, and neither did the right wing. When it opened at the Edinburgh Festival it was not very well reviewed, and at the Royal Court it was a failure.

During this low period, unbeknownst to me, a battle had been raging between Spyros Skouras and the heads of Twentieth Century–Fox on the one hand and Walter Wanger and Elizabeth Taylor on the other. Walter had started making the film of *Cleopatra* in Rome, and he and Elizabeth wanted me for the part of Caesar, while the studio was dead against it. Well, Walter and Elizabeth won and the studio lost, thanks to Elizabeth's tenacity and also to Joseph Mankiewicz belatedly coming in as the new director of the film.

When I was offered the part of Caesar I asked George Devine for a release from the Nigel Dennis play. The four weeks of the run were not up, but we were doing very little business. George was understanding but angry; he thought it would be bad for Nigel Dennis' reputation if the play closed so soon.

Here again, I think I was overhasty because I was in a muddled state of mind. I should have considered more carefully where my allegiance lay. Certainly today I would not be in such a hurry but would tell the film company to wait until I had worked out my obligation to play and playwright. However George—being George—did release me, on condition that I help finance the next production at the Royal Court, and I began forthwith trying on togas.

Cleopatra

My first day of shooting on *Cleopatra* took place in the Forum, where I stood to make my opening address to the Roman Senate, immediately before Cleopatra's spectacular entry into Rome.

The Forum had been reconstructed at Cinecittà, and hordes of extras waited outside the studio gates that morning: six thousand of them, hired for the big day, with their group leaders who had been practicing for weeks. Italian elephants had already proved too temperamental, and a team of milder-mannered elephants had been imported from England. Other wild animals and hundreds of horses had all been drilled in preparation for their roles in the procession which heralded Cleopatra's arrival, with Caesarion, riding on a huge black sphinx drawn by slaves.

There were two starting signals, two rockets—one to signify that we were filming, the second to tell me to begin on my speech. I waited for the second rocket, clad in the purple toga, with the crown of oak leaves on my head. I had learned the speech in depth, but even so it was going to be difficult launching into Caesar with no breaking-in time, filming in the open air, with a fresh wind blowing and the commotion

179

of all those animals in the background. Among the senators gathered around for the great moment there were many familiar faces: Kenneth Haigh, Roddy McDowall, Michael Hordern, Hume Cronyn, Robert Stephens . . . I looked away from them and concentrated on the speech:

CAESAR (*for the benefit of all*): Queen Cleopatra has most graciously had golden medals struck off to commemorate this great occasion—for each of our distinguished senators, each medal inscribed with the name of him for whom it is intended—

Imagine starting on those lines at full voice while six thousand people, at ten dollars each per day, milled around in the background, and while my delighted friends the senators sat there watching me! I think it was the "of him for whom" which foxed me. The script continued:

ANTONY (*playing along*): A most thoughtful and generous gesture, Caesar! I am proud to wear mine . . .

CAESAR: And I! But I am displeased to see that so few of our colleagues share that pride! Is this to be Her Majesty's first taste of Roman hospitality—is the outstretched hand of our approaching guest to be slighted by her Roman host?

The senators, many of whom had known me all my acting life, were enchanted: all day long, "displeased" or not, I fluffed the majestic words which the director, Joe Mankiewicz, had written himself, and which he wanted me to have letter-perfect. Again and again the animals, and the six thousand extras, were turned around and sent back to the starting line, and after the huge cannonball pats of elephants' dung were cleaned up, we would start again—only for me to forget my lines again.

Finally, as the sun was going down, Leon Shamroy said, "The light is going very red, Joe, I don't think we can go on."

The next day, on the first try, I got through the speech successfully. Later in the day, when I had been able to get my bearings in this enormous scene, I asked Joe, "What

With Elizabeth Taylor
in *Cleopatra*
(20th Century–Fox)

happened to the zebras we were promised in the parade?"

Joe said that they were not zebras, but were to have been donkeys painted with stripes. He added, giving me a funny look, "They forgot their lines."

The work on the triumphal procession went on for days, until the rains came. It gave the extras an opportunity to learn their way around. Hundreds of them collected their togas early in the morning and hid them somewhere on the set, while they popped over the wall and went back to their work in the city. At the end of the day they returned to Cinecittà and climbed in over the wall to pick up their togas and their daily ten dollars. And still we didn't get to Cleopatra's big entrance. The weather closed down, and the Forum was flooded.

It was in fact seven months later that we completed that piece of filming, with the three hundred gold-painted slaves drawing on the sphinx, and Cleopatra kneeling before Caesar, and winking. Elizabeth Taylor, I think, suffers from vertigo, and they had a terrible time getting her down a steep flight of steps into the Forum. It was extraordinary to think, as I watched them coaxing her down, how many months had elapsed between fluffing my lines and Cleopatra's actual arrival, and to recall how I had felt during that first opening scene. Sometimes all the uncertainties of youth come back to us, and we are like children again, and I had felt myself back in the shoes of the spotty gangling boy at the Liverpool Repertory, unable to say, "Fetch a doctor . . . baby . . ." All the experience, all the life that has gone before, is wiped out, and for all our exterior self-assurance we are inwardly back at Square One. It took me a little time to regain my confidence because I could not at first catch hold of the Hollywood bluff to shake it by the neck, as Elizabeth could, and as Richard Burton later learned to do.

Cleopatra was a fantastic undertaking, in terms not only of money but of nervous energy and time. The producer, Walter Wanger, invested some five years in this film, and many of the technicians worked on it for two or three years.

The actors endured long spells of waiting. Richard Burton, for one, didn't work for several months after he arrived in Rome. I know Fox had bought him out of a very successful run in *Camelot,* at considerable cost, and it must have been miserable for him, hanging around with nothing to do. I remember that at one point he contemplated slipping away to make a television show in New York. And for me too it was one of those hurry-up-and-wait situations. Normally I tend to procrastinate when an offer comes along—it drives everybody else mad and me too, but in the midst of all the bustle it is important to me to stand still and explore what is suggested, and then, if necessary, withdraw. This time I dived right in and got to Rome much too early and had to wait about for nearly two months, for scripts.

I suppose *Cleopatra* was among the first of a long series of very big and extremely expensive Hollywood epics, a genre of film quite different from those I'd made in Hollywood in the Forties. The films made in the Sixties were designed to hit the public between the eyes, and above all to get them out of their houses, away from the dreaded television set. They were designed along the lines of a great theatrical event, with a fifteen-minute intermission, and they were called "road shows."

For those big spectacular films the producers discovered that a new technique had to be found. In the old films, the close-up was really all that mattered, and actors accordingly learned close-up acting; it didn't matter what size or shape they were, you hardly knew whether they were tall or short. With the advent of the wide screen film makers had to come back to the theatre actors, who knew how to move, and project, and how to use their voices, as on the stage. In these big films the actor was in medium shot most of the time—visible from the waist up—and he couldn't hug the mike or disguise his stature. This was one reason why, for *Cleopatra,* they came to Richard Burton and myself.

Though they had developed new techniques of filming, the studios had yet to change their style of management. Much publicity was given to Elizabeth Taylor's fee for the film, variously reported to have been one million dollars, or two million dollars; but most of the blame for extravagant expenditure attached to Twentieth Century–Fox's own handling of the production.

It began in September, 1958, when Walter Wanger went to Twentieth Century–Fox to make *Cleopatra,* thinking he would have the same autonomy there that he had enjoyed at other studios—his first words with Spyros Skouras, the Greek-American president of Fox, were about filming *Cleopatra,* and he had already made up his mind that only Elizabeth Taylor could fill the role properly. "Who needs a Liz Taylor?" asked Fox, but eventually they themselves discovered that they needed a Liz Taylor, and it was Elizabeth's turn to put off signing her contract, partly in order to show Skouras that he could not control everyone. She also explained to Skouras that she preferred to deal directly with Walter Wanger, "because he was honest."

Liz had a wonderful way with Hollywood executives of the old school. As a child actress she had had a rough time, and learned about studio politics the hard way. While working on *Cleopatra,* she excelled herself in this respect, and she had quite a considerable influence on many decisions.

For one thing, she fought the old Hollywood brigade to get me into the picture. The two actors he wouldn't have in the film, Skouras declared, were Richard Burton and Harrison. Burton meant nothing at the box office, I was box-office poison—nearly all movie stars have bouts of this ailment, and though it is largely an imaginary condition dreamt up by the old brigade, it sometimes kills off actors who don't have the stage to return to. What Skouras was really saying, of course, was that he was afraid that Richard Burton and I might be expensive, and too independent-minded. Anyone who showed signs of independence was labeled "No good at the box office."

If I had been *au fait* with the production problems on

Cleopatra up to the time when I was asked to play Caesar, I might not have been so eager to accept. As it was, I arrived at Cinecittà to find Joseph Mankiewicz working nights and Sundays on the script. When we started the shooting in Italy he had the job only half completed. While we made the first half he was still writing the second. There was no opportunity to see a script in advance, but having worked with Joe before I knew and respected his almost brutal refusal to be side-tracked from whatever he set out to achieve. There's only one other person I would take on professional trust like that, and that is Carol Reed.

People tend to think that a film that has cost all that money and has had so much publicity can only be a supercolossal joke. But it's not. *Cleopatra* is a serious attempt to throw new light on one of the greatest stories in history. Mankiewicz had read everyone on the subject, from Plutarch and Suetonius to Shakespeare and Shaw, and could not be faulted on the smallest detail. His principal problem was that after the drama of Caesar's tremendous relationship with Cleopatra, in the first half of the story, it was difficult for the second part, with Antony, not to be an anticlimax. Antony had been Caesar's faithful lieutenant, his right hand, and he could not fail to feel overshadowed by Caesar's ghost. This Joe illustrated by depicting Mark Antony as an eccentric and a heavy drinker, who thinks he has won Cleopatra, whereas in fact Cleopatra has taken possession of him. I differed with Joe on only one point: I could never quite believe that Caesar, with all the political and military problems that were on his mind at the time, could have been so absolutely obsessed with Cleopatra. It seemed out of character, and I resisted as much as possible the pressure to play him that way.

Caesar was far more difficult for me than, say, Higgins. There are not so many dimensions to Higgins, who was practically Shaw: a dictatorial, humorful misogynist. When you have to play someone like Caesar there are all kinds of extra difficulties, because he was such a great man. You have to find out, somehow, what were the component parts that made him great, be they good or bad. I think that unless you are a real character actor, and practically put on a mask, you must bring the role into yourself as much as you can. I could bring Higgins into myself, because I'm more akin to him than I could at first feel to Caesar; but I think I succeeded, up to a point, with Caesar too.

I did not look much like the generally accepted image of Caesar, who was short and tubby and dynamic, and there was no point in trying to. My makeup man was De Rossi, a great artist, whom I have worked with since, and we experimented with all sorts of wigs and costumes.

The first time Rachel saw me in wig and costume she immediately started to laugh, saying I looked like a Martian. The costume was an extraordinary affair of horrible red velvet, and my face, apparently, didn't have a single line on it. Rachel quite rightly wondered what on earth they were up to, and I suspected that under the wig they must have given my face a lift in some way. But I had to test the clothes and makeup anyway, so I went through with the test, the results of which seemed to me, too, to be very funny. When later I saw Mankiewicz in the Grand Hotel, where he and I were staying, I asked him to take a look at the tests. He came back to me asking indignantly, "What happened to your face?"

I told him I thought they must have given it a lift, and he said, "All those lines and things, I *want* all of those lines."

I did too, so we started again from scratch.

While we were having the clothes made, I learned in some detail about the dyes used in Caesar's day, which rather fascinated me, and discovered that the violent hue of red that they had dressed me in originally bore no resemblance to any of the dyes that could conceivably have existed at that time. The Romans had used a marvelous red dye made from terracotta, and a purple dye which came from fish. The purple, of course, was used for the robe that Caesar wore on state occasions—he alone, I think, was allowed to wear purple at that period.

Irene Sharaff was designing Elizabeth Taylor's clothes, and I think it was she who did some excellent costume designs for me, which worked out very well. They were pleated, and they were in the right colors.

Richard Burton was rather less fussy about his costumes, as I remember. I was sitting with him one day waiting to start a scene, and he kept on grumbling about his boots and how uncomfortable they were. I had had my boots made there in Rome, and they were marvelously comfortable, and I asked who had made his boots. Nobody had made his boots, Richard said, they were Stephen Boyd's boots, left over from the attempt at making the film in London, when Stephen Boyd was playing Mark Antony. It hadn't even occurred to Richard to see that he had boots of his own—typical of Richard, he doesn't worry much about such things.

Once we had survived my disastrous start in the opening scene in the Forum, and the floods of October, the first three months of shooting went fairly smoothly. We made an average of at least two minutes' film a day, which was not bad, considering the elaborate sets and the number of people in some of the scenes. The bulk of the first half of the picture—though by no means all of it—was done, I should say, in three to four months.

Working with Elizabeth Taylor was rather like being a very well-trained hundred-yard sprinter, waiting in the starting position for the gun to go off. Sometimes one had to wait in that position for several hours; clad in a toga, it was harder even than in shorts. Finally, she would show up, and there would be loud cries of "Lights!" The sets had to be lit, and the scene hastily re-rehearsed which had been prepared the night before, and then shot as soon as possible.

It always seemed to me a huge added expense, in an already costly film, to give so much time to waiting, and preparing, and lighting those vast sets, instead of concentrating on rehearsals with the actors. But the other factor that contributed to the delays was that we were using a film process called Todd-AO. It had been invented by Elizabeth Taylor's late husband, Michael Todd, who was killed in a plane crash in 1958, and it produced a very large film, both in height and in width. As the sets covered by this very large negative were correspondingly enormous, it took literally hours to light up all those myriad nooks and crannies.

I think Elizabeth is one of the most professional actresses I've ever met. When she arrives to do a scene, she knows exactly what she wants to do with it, and one has to be ready for her, to keep up with her. She's always word-perfect, too, and she has a photographic memory as far as lines are concerned. There are ways and ways of learning parts—having had a theatre training, I can only learn my lines slowly and in depth, memorizing them so that they stay in the mind for weeks and months, possibly even years, but for the cinema it is quite feasible to learn them quickly and lightly, off the top of your head. This may be the better way to learn lines for the screen, so that once you've played the scene you can forget them again.

The film's management continued to oscillate between unseemly extravagance and false economies. On one occasion I came back from a trip to London to find the cost cutters hard at work and my chauffeur up in arms. He was a particularly nice man, rather unusual in that he was a Protestant Italian, from an old Huguenot family. He was so obviously upset that I asked him what was the matter, and he told me the studio was refusing to pay his bill, and that he had only come to meet me out of personal loyalty.

I arrived at the studio the next day and found that I had a new dressing room too, a small and poky room tucked away over one of the sound stages. My trailer dressing room on the set had been taken away—the trailer in which I sat and worked on my lines, and spent my day, and without which I would have been lost.

I called Walter Wanger and Sid Rogell, the costing man, to my dungeon, and said I had no intention of getting into costume, or of working another minute, if my chauffeur wasn't paid and my trailer returned. Then I ordered them out of my dungeon and sat back to await results. As Elizabeth had found, these tactics produced results. After a half day wasted, the chauffeur was paid and the trailer brought back. I later heard that Sid Rogell had just then been promoted, and that I'd had the temerity to berate one of Skouras' innumerable "presidents and heads of studio."

In January, 1962, Elizabeth began shooting her first scenes with Richard, and then, as everybody knows, the balloon went up. We had by then shot some two-thirds of Caesar's half of the picture, and after Mark Antony had made his début with Cleopatra, my scenes were kept in reserve, in case of catastrophe. If they could not shoot on either Elizabeth or Richard, I was the stopgap who could be called in to work, so that they need not close the studios. Catastrophes, of course, were happening all the time.

I knew they had all the second half of the picture to do, and I soon tired of being a stopgap. Rachel was in England making *This Sporting Life*, the film for which she won the British Film Academy Award. I thought my present situation was rather ridiculous and decided not to stand for it, and without telling anybody went off to Beaconsfield, where Rachel was making the picture, to spend a few days with her.

She was thoroughly disenchanted with the Hollywood scene —as indeed was I by all the shenanigans—and was enjoying working with Lindsay Anderson and Richard Harris on what turned out to be a splendid and touching film.

While I was in England I drove down to Poole to try out a new speedboat in the Solent. I came back into harbor to find people waving from the pier at me and wondered what this reception could mean. It meant, alas, that Cinecittà had been on the telephone, ordering me to go back at once as there had been another catastrophe. In Rome the next morning I found them all very angry with me for taking French leave.

In March, when I had time off, Rachel and I were married

in Genoa. We had a civil wedding conducted by a man called Machiavelli, wearing a beautiful large sash. After that it was back to the grind again in Rome, endlessly waiting for the occasional call to come, to play one or another of my remaining scenes; it was very irksome, because I had to keep them brushed up and ready to go.

Finally the thing drew to a close. At least, I drew to a close in the thing. Elizabeth and Richard went off to Ischia to do some of the sea battles, and I was released.

Twentieth Century–Fox had been threatening for a long time to make do without the Philippi and Pharsalia scenes, for reasons of economy, but when they ran the picture they realized that they would have to have a big battle scene for the beginning of the film. So it was that the opening shots of Cleopatra, that stunning sequence in which Caesar defeats Pompey, were the last frames to be filmed.

Through rains and floods we trekked down to the south of Spain, to Almería, where the landscape is all tufa rock and looks as though it has only just emerged from under the sea, and there we did battle with a vast collection of cavalry, and all sorts of Roman weapons of war.

While we were shooting in Almería, Joe Mankiewicz came to see me and asked if I had a "likeness clause" in my contract. I'd never heard of a likeness clause, but Joe said he had a rough idea by then of the way the billing seemed to be going, and it was obvious that the studios wanted to capitalize on all the scandalmongering about Richard Burton and Elizabeth Taylor, and hoped to sell the picture by playing up the romance. He suggested that I look into my contract and see if I had such a clause.

My agents confirmed that I did have a likeness clause, which stipulated that whenever Richard's name or picture was used in advertisements for Cleopatra, my name or picture had to appear beside his and be given equal prominence. It is in fact a standard clause in actors' contracts, but I hadn't heard of it before. Mankiewicz had come across it because Bogart

Great Caesar's ghost

had invoked it when he was excluded from the billing of Mankiewicz's film *The Barefoot Contessa,* in which he starred with Ava Gardner.

Having found out that we had those rights, my agents put Fox on warning. Fox ignored this, and sure enough a huge billboard soon appeared on Broadway, showing the two lovers together, with no sign of Caesar. My lawyers weighed in with a suit. For some time, nothing much was heard from Fox, and I left the problem for the lawyers to thrash out between them. Then I was told that a very strange thing had occurred on Broadway. Men had been seen climbing the scaffolding, and sticking up a minute picture of Caesar in one corner of this gigantic poster, so that it now looked like a postcard with a stamp in the corner. This caused a furor, and much laughter; it looked ridiculous, and still did not answer to my contractual rights.

It took a great many more letters from my lawyers to Fox pointing out that this wasn't the intention of a likeness clause, before Caesar was reinstated, and posters appeared with him and Antony sitting on either side of Cleopatra.

It was an ignominious, farcical business even though I got my "rights" in the end. I disliked the fact that I had literally to fight for a footing in what was a three-handed film, particularly when the other two were friends as well as colleagues. It wasn't their fault in any way.

Richard and Elizabeth came to stay with me at the villa in Portofino for several weeks when the film was over. We used to go up to my hilltop bistro above the house and I think we all enjoyed the peace and relaxation (as well as the local wine and spaghetti Genovese) looking up into the olive trees and out to the distant sea.

When Richard and Elizabeth left, I settled down to lick my wounds and recoup.

CHAPTER ELEVEN

"Just You Wait, Henry Higgins"

A T Portofino I awaited the next moves on the proposed film of *My Fair Lady*. Jack Warner had bought this property from CBS at a large price, and it was to be his swan song, the last film he would produce himself in his own studio— the last of the Mohicans, and a fine one at that.

The English newspapers, which arrived a day late in Portofino, told of a battle royal being waged for the part of Professor Higgins. It was, obviously, the plum part of the decade, and it was said that the great stars were actually writing in and asking if they could do a test for it.

I too wanted the part, but I was not going to press matters. The best way to get a part I've always thought is to pretend not to be interested in it. And though I got an Academy Award nomination for playing Julius Caesar in *Cleopatra*, I had heard that the film moguls were saying, "Rex looks old." Certainly I looked old: I was playing a man in his latter days, and an epileptic to boot—not a bounding juvenile.

I also knew that in the film industry of that time it was not considered safe to take a stage actor, which was what I was then quite rightly seen to be, for the same role on film. It had been tried on a few occasions, usually with disastrous results.

So I spent the spring in Portofino, skimming the day-old newspapers, and busied myself building a garden house and a Roman bath on a terrace surrounded by olive trees. The bath I had designed like a miniature amphitheatre, in which one could stand at the center or sit and talk, drinking the wine from our own vineyards. It was made of Carrara marble, with a mosaic of stones around it, and, like the garden house, it was designed by Arthur Barbosa, whose own cottage near Tunbridge Wells has come over the years to resemble a miniature Versailles. Elizabeth Taylor saw his designs and fell in love with them, so I wasted no time in getting Arthur down to talk to the Burtons, and he was commissioned to refurbish their yacht.

The Battle for Higgins continued. George Cukor, the director, flew to the Middle East to take a look at Peter O'Toole, who was then making *Lawrence of Arabia*. Cary Grant was approached, and told Warners: "Not only will I not play Higgins, if you don't put Rex Harrison in it, I won't go and see it." My advisers suggested that I come down off the top of my hill and show my face, perhaps drop in on Hollywood to visit friends, but I maintained that if they wanted me they would come to me; they had seen me do the part on the stage, and it was up to them. I sat tight, just as, though I didn't know it at the time, Jack Warner was sitting tight.

Then, one evening, just as we were about to retire—everybody goes to bed early up there on top of my hill—the phone rang, and it was George Cukor. The lines from Portofino to California are not the best, but through the crackles I gathered that he was asking me, rather tentatively, to go to Hollywood to do a photographic test for Higgins. I was much tickled by this request. I said, "Absolutely not. If you want me to play it, then I'll come," and hung up.

Then I found two Polaroid photos which had been taken on the boat, in which I appeared stark naked, in one of them holding a Chianti bottle in front of me, in the other reading a strategically placed copy of the *New Statesman*. I

194

amused myself by sending these to George Cukor with a covering note: "If you want a photographic test, this is it." I don't know why it was—perhaps because I was very thin at the time, and George may have been expecting to find me quite decrepit—but for whatever reason, those pictures appealed to him. The studios telephoned and said I had the part and promised to return the photographs to me intact.

I had to go on playing hard to get while the agents hammered out the details of the contract, but finally I set off for California. With me I took my Rolls-Royce, feeling that it might, in times of stress, boost my morale; I took it over on the boat and had it driven across America, so that when I flew into Los Angeles I was met at the airport by my own car.

After a brief stay at the Bel Air Hotel I found a house near the Warner Brothers studios. It belonged to two male decorators, and was quite pretty, but false. It had a tennis court which was much too short, and a lot of very modern rooms with great glass windows built around the pool, thus depriving the occupants of pool and bedrooms of all privacy.

One day when I was standing by the pool, just about to go and record one of my numbers, my agent, Jack Clayton, arrived. He saw me by the pool and came toward me, straight through one of those plate-glass windows. He went on walking, thank God, because behind him the glass came down like stalactites. He quite literally did not know what had hit him; he was untouched, not a spot of blood on him, but as white as a sheet. The shattered glass landed on an enormous table, which the two decorators had told us was very rare ancient Egyptian work; it cracked and crumbled and disintegrated into a heap of rather modern-looking cement. We replaced the table, quite easily, from a shop in Beverly Hills—Jack had to be restored with half a bottle of brandy.

I was out in California for the best part of a year. Since *My Fair Lady* was Jack Warner's own production he put his heart and soul into it. Of all the film moguls Jack Warner was the one I got along with best, long before I made any films for him. They called him The Colonel, in Hollywood. He had an enormous amount of energy, and he always made me laugh, and dictator though he was he disguised it with jokes and quips.

The sets, which were built and ready to rehearse on, took up practically the whole of the Warner Brothers lot, except that Sinatra had a deal with Warners at the time, and while we were making *My Fair Lady* made two or three films with his buddies—Sammy Davis, Jr., and Dean Martin and the group. They used to drive around the studios in golf carts, all cheery and carefree, and I wished I were able to join the party.

Cecil Beaton designed the costumes for *My Fair Lady,* and collaborated with Gene Allen on the sets, but he did not often show himself. He had crossed swords with Cukor on goodness knows what matter, and used to hibernate in a cottage, surrounded by the wardrobe ladies and materials. One of his rare appearances on set was during the Ascot scene, when he arrived immaculately dressed, with a card around his neck saying, "I have laryngitis." He never spoke, but gesticulated incessantly. He wore a large, white, Stetsonlike hat, and a white suit with a flower in the buttonhole.

Audrey Hepburn was playing Eliza Doolittle, partly because she was one of the now rare actresses who could command a million dollars for each picture, and Jack Warner somehow thought this guaranteed his investment. Cukor was not backward in pointing out to me how lucky I was to be acting with a million-dollar girl. It was in no way Audrey's design that she, and not Julie Andrews, was chosen for the film role; it was the luck of the draw and she had a tough time over it. She was not allowed to sing the score, although she dearly wanted to, and unfortunately it became widely known that her numbers were dubbed. I think this may have been why she was not even nominated for an Academy Award, because in my opinion she gave a superb performance.

There are very few similarities between the two girls, except that they both have extraordinary charm. Julie had been discovered, by Val Parnell, when she was still very young, and had been a theatrical person probably ever since she could remember, with a whole covey of agents and managers pushing her on and hanging on to her coattails. Throughout the run of *My Fair Lady,* onstage we had had an extremely good working relationship, leading separate private lives and meeting only onstage. She was brought up in the theatre, to be independent and self-reliant and all the other things that the theatre demands of you, and I think there's a lot of steel in her, more steel than in Audrey. Audrey's background was different. She is Dutch and was brought up outside the theatre and, I believe, once wanted to be a ballet dancer. She came to London and went to the same dancing school as my late wife, Kay, before doing a series of small film roles. It was the French novelist Colette who discovered her for her first starring part in *Gigi.*

She is a very gentle and sweet person, and we get on very well. She was terribly thin, and in the habit of eating only raw vegetables, which I always thought could not give her enough energy. She gave me a red bicycle to ride around the lot on, with a place in front for my script, like the one Fred Astaire had given her with a place up front for her Yorkshire terrier, Muffin.

It was very good to be working once again with Stanley Holloway, and altogether we had a very distinguished cast. I had a new mother in Gladys Cooper, an old friend; and Wilfrid Hyde-White, a beautifully sardonic fellow whom I seem to have known most of my life, played Pickering. In eastern climes he always seemed to be freezing to death, and wore a splendid overcoat with an astrakhan collar, but California suited him better, and best of all Palm Springs, where I believe he now has a house.

We rehearsed for six weeks before we turned a foot of film, and it was quite a painful business. Though I was trying to adapt the material from stage terms to film terms, I did at least know it, whereas Audrey was feeling her way through a show she didn't know. I don't know how she managed it, though Cukor of course is a past master at coaxing the best out of female stars. He has had the knack ever since he worked with Garbo on her early successes.

It was some years since I had played *My Fair Lady* at Drury Lane, a long enough period in which to dissociate myself from the play, but still I found the whole pattern of the show coming back to me as a theatrical performance. I was always conscious of this, and fought it continuously. The intimacy of the screen requires quite different acting techniques from those of the theatre. I had to think out the performance in front of the cameras and not, as in the theatre, project it.

We shot for about four months, which is quite a short schedule for this type of film, and I developed my own technique for doing the musical numbers. Warner Brothers, after all, was the first studio to produce sound movies, as I knew only too well from my touring days, and I insisted on doing the numbers live, instead of prerecording them and then mouthing them to my playback on the set, which was the usual practice in musicals. As I knew the numbers so very well it was perfectly feasible for me to do them live on the set, as long as the director used the two-camera technique to provide for both long shots and close-ups.

In order to go right through the numbers without stopping I had to use a neck mike, a shortwave radio microphone slung around my neck under my clothes. They are used quite a lot in cabarets now, but then was the first time they had been used in a film studio. I did the first two numbers with this mike before the studio had permission from Washington to use this type of device. We kept picking up all sorts of things on the same wavelength, including taxi drivers and the mayor of Miami—no wonder Washington was worried. Often we would have a good take right through a number, only to have the sound people confess that they had picked up a radio-

With Audrey Hepburn while filming *My Fair Lady*
(Warner Brothers)

phone conversation, so that we would have to go through the whole thing again.

George Cukor still works in front of the camera, much more like a stage director. I know film directors who only look through the camera and hardly ever look anywhere else. They frame a performance and see it as film. Cukor never looks through the camera, nor is he a man to let things go. He stretches actors to their limits and will not let them rely on technique or take the easy way out. He also knew when we were working a scene into the ground, when to make us break off and come back again the next morning.

The things he did for me were quite remarkable. I had a lot of trouble, for instance, with the last number, "I've Grown Accustomed to Her Face." On the stage the whole show leads up to this number, but for the film I was doing it cold, and this I found very difficult, as indeed it has been whenever I have had to do "Accustomed to Her Face" on its own, for charity shows or royal performances. I think that number needs the whole weight of the show behind it to give proper significance to the moment when Higgins suddenly realizes that he has fallen in love with Liza.

We spent a morning trying, and failing, to get it right and I retired to my dressing room for lunch feeling pretty desperate. I stood at the window and watched the gang in their golf carts whizzing past, singing and laughing without a care in the world. I decided I was trying too hard, and that we had set the number rather too firmly in my moves and the camera moves.

Whereupon George simply dispensed with further rehearsal and said, "Feel totally free. Whatever you do, the camera will follow you, so do what you like." And that was what happened. That is where the Hollywood cameramen are absolutely incredible—the camera moved when I moved, while I did what I felt like, and thanks to the skill of those technicians it was all in focus and all correctly timed.

At the end of the number, moreover, I had to climb a flight

of steps to go into my house, and in order to leave me free, Cukor placed a camera ready there, without anybody behind it, and left it running throughout the number. When I walked into the shot there was nobody within two hundred feet of me, and I was able to finish the number and go into the house without distraction and without stopping. Cukor understood that this number needed to be done in one continuous line, right through to the end, and so found a way of doing it. Altogether I found him a masterly director.

During these months of very taxing work, Rachel's mother and father flew out to stay for a while, to keep her company. Rachel's father was very frail: it had been discovered, while I was still making *Cleopatra,* that he had a stomach cancer, which through the good offices of my friend Dr. Goldman had been successfully removed. It had been a clean operation, but at seventy, naturally, his recovery was slow.

Rachel was restless and unhappy. I think she could enjoy the fleshpots as much as I, but felt a deep need to earn them. She had burning ambition, great talent, and enormous energy, and felt she was wasting her days when she was not working.

She took some solace, however, in a visit from our friend Lindsay Anderson, for whom she had worked so successfully in the past. And she got on with David Selznick, a man who, in the great days of Hollywood, had had a great many dealings with women, and coped with their idiosyncrasies with a kindness which I perhaps lacked.

I had met David when he was married to Irene Selznick, who is herself a dynamo and who did a great deal, I think, to help him in his public life. But it was while I was doing *My Fair Lady* in California that I really got to know him. By then he had not made a film for about ten years, but he lived as if he were still the head of a studio. He had his own telegraphic systems and a whole gaggle of secretaries, and moved in the grand world and collected around him an unusual and brilliant cross section of people. Tower House, on top of one

201

of the Beverly Hills, became a mecca to Huxley, Isherwood, and Auden, to Arthur Miller and Marilyn Monroe, to the French director Renoir, as well as to the younger generation of up-and-coming actors.

David was a marvelous man—a giant, who had become so involved with his second wife, Jennifer Jones, so besotted, that he couldn't develop any property without trying to include her in it. He had had great imagination and immense talent as a producer, and he still had an awful lot of films in him. He was fascinated by Joseph Conrad's novels and talked to me about many films that he wanted to make with me—and Jennifer.

While we were in Hollywood, I acquired an agreeable addition to the household. We had occasional visits from a neighboring basset called William; he was casual and outrageously stubborn, and yet courteous and loving, and I fell in love with the breed and determined to have one of my own. I started a long search for basset puppies and drove sometimes for hundreds of miles on weekends when I heard of a litter for sale. But the puppies advertised were generally not quite bassets, which are a cross between a bloodhound and some low-slung hound—now extinct—first bred in northern France three hundred years ago. They have great fat front paws for digging, because their job was to go underground, in the sandy stretches north of Paris, seeking out large rodents. The true basset has a long tail which he holds erect when he is on the scent, with a white tip designed to show up in the low bush in which the dog was bred to hunt.

I found a litter at last in the San Fernando Valley, where a Mrs. Smiley bred French bassets. I picked out my favorite and called him Homer, and he is still with me, loving and crafty. He has been joined by Tara and Jason, and among them they take up a lot of room.

I found that with the filming of *My Fair Lady* a lot of my old buoyancy had returned. After the buffeting and the uncertainties of *Cleopatra,* it was a joy to find a setup organized

With Anthony Asquith on the set of *The Yellow Rolls-Royce*
(Norman Hargood)

almost as in the theatre. We had done something worthwhile, and done it well, and when I went to London to do *The Yellow Rolls-Royce* I was on top of the world.

The script for *The Yellow Rolls-Royce* was written by Terence Rattigan, and this was the first time Terry and I had worked together since *French Without Tears*—extraordinary really, because we had seen each other constantly, over the twenty-eight years that intervened, on one side of the Atlantic or the other. Once again I found it a joy to speak his lines.

The producer was Anatole de Grunwald, who was a great friend, affectionately known as Tolly de Greenteeth, and the

203

director was the great Anthony Asquith, nicknamed Puffin, who had been the first really outstanding director in the British film industry. His gentle touch and his steel, under the gentleness, when he wanted to get some effect he wasn't getting from a scene were a joy to watch. He was always enormously courteous, and confessed that in the film studios, which are littered with wires and large squishy pipes, he constantly found himself apologizing to the pipes when he stepped on them, thinking they were somebody's feet. *The Yellow Rolls-Royce* was the last film he made, and I was fortunate to have had the opportunity to work with him even once.

My leading lady was Jeanne Moreau. She is a wondrous actress, and such fun to work with—everything seemed to go right between us, without effort or strain. I began to think that some of the film experiences I had had before *My Fair Lady* were just bad dreams.

Little did I know what was to come.

While I was still making *My Fair Lady*, I had been persuaded, against my better judgment, to make a film for Twentieth Century–Fox called *The Agony and the Ecstasy,* with Charlton Heston. It was an epic about Michelangelo and Pope Julius, a huge canvas indeed, and was to be directed by my old friend from the Home Guard days, Carol Reed.

I don't think Carol was himself. I think Charlton Heston was absolutely himself, and by the end I didn't know who I was. Pope I knew I was, though the real star was Michelangelo, and Heston very politely and very nicely made me feel that it was extremely kind of me to be supporting him. Carol did little to disabuse him of this notion, so I did everything I could to make myself believe that the picture was about Pope Julius rather than about Michelangelo.

In this I was not too successful. Heston is an enormously tall man—if I am six foot one, he must be about six foot three —and I asked my wardrobe man, as I was wearing long robes, to put a little lift in my shoes, so that I could gain a couple of inches, and meet Heston at his own level. The lifts were duly put in, and I eyed Heston and congratulated myself that at least he no longer towered above me. As the film went on, however, it seemed to me that he was growing. Eyeball to eyeball he was once more a couple of inches taller than I. I looked down at his feet—not a sign of lifts! He must have grown through sheer tenacity. Neither of us made any comment, nor did our wardrobe men—it was a very funny, silent contest.

A lot of the work was done on location in Perugia, and in a village called Todi, and in castles north of Rome, as well as in the De Laurentiis studio, where we rebuilt the Sistine Chapel. The filming was laborious, and at one point Carol asked me an extraordinary question: "Rex, do you always work as hard as this?" We hadn't worked together since 1939, and it was then 1964. I said, "Yes, I do work. I think about the part, I work." Carol said it was incredible; I think he was surprised to find me so professional. I found it weird that he didn't realize the amount of work that had gone on between 1939 and 1964.

I took a house near the Via Appia Antica, just outside the walls of Rome, which is to my mind one of the most spooky and depressing roads that I've ever trodden. It has seen too much tragedy and horror, ever since the Romans began marching up and down there; so many people have died there that the place is heavy with ghosts. Our house came complete with a crypt, and when this was opened up for visiting archaeologists, my two Angora cats took one sniff of the unpleasant atmosphere and puffed themselves up into big furry balls of anger and fear. It was a crypt which seemed to have covered a long period because there were both the ashes of dead bodies of a pre-Christian era and the bones of the post-Christian era. Anyway, nothing you would want in your garden.

Rachel was working in England and was away a lot of the time, and when I wasn't actually filming, I walked Rome from wall to wall. Every capital city has a different quality. Paris is open and beautiful and, underlying its mercenary

"After *The Agony* was over I had to go back to New York for the premiere of *My Fair Lady*." Rex as Pope Julius and as Henry Higgins

attitude to tourists, it enjoys a real gaiety and sense of fun. London is a unique collection of villages that just happen to be connected up with one another, each area with its own shops, its own church, its own individual character. But Rome, to me, has an air of evil hanging over it. I know the city well, and it is small and somehow very limiting. I'm probably prejudiced because it brings back less than ecstatic memories of the filming of *Cleopatra*.

After *The Agony* was over I had to go to New York for the opening of *My Fair Lady* in November, 1964. Jack Warner, George Cukor, Audrey Hepburn, Cecil Beaton, and I went after New York to Chicago and Los Angeles by private plane. It was an enormously enjoyable, happy trip. Each opening was for some major charity with a ball and reception afterward. We were all very proud of the film and delighted with its enormous reception. In Los Angeles we were hailed as victors by the industry and wined and dined very lavishly. I inwardly blushed at all the things I had said about Hollywood drawing rooms when I found myself firmly ensconced in them again.

Rachel, who had not accompanied me on the tour, was in London. I flew back and we spent Christmas in Portofino before attending the premieres of *My Fair Lady* in London and Paris in January. I then learned to my delight that I had been nominated for an Academy Award. I had been nominated for it the year before for Caesar—the year Sidney Poitier won it—and the Academy was anxious that I should be present in case I got it this year, so they paid my expenses out to California where I arrived in March.

As always the buzz before Academy Award night was at its height. It was a strange evening. I knew that if I won the award I would be on the stage with two Fair Ladies. Julie had been nominated (for her role in *Mary Poppins*); Audrey had not, but she was in Hollywood to present the awards to the winners. Well, it all happened. I won it and Julie won it and things were fairly hectic backstage trying to keep the factions in the right place for photographs and interviews. The public-relations people had a difficult time, but they are well equipped for this.

After all the brouhaha was over we stayed in New York, and there what turned out to be a rather unfortunate occurrence took place. Unfortunate from many angles; it was roads taken and not taken all over again. Joe Mankiewicz came to the hotel with a large suitcase. It contained a script, very long and unfinished, but his next project. He had not worked since *Cleopatra* two years before and was very hesitant about

The night of the Oscar: with Jack Warner and Gladys Cooper

showing me any of it, but he was very persuasive in that he wanted me to play the leading part.

Joe's powers of persuasion are very great, and after a couple of hours of producing odd scenes like rabbits out of a hat, he had me hooked. After all, I had taken *Cleopatra* on trust because it was Joe, why not this? Oh dear! It had as many titles as delays. When I agreed to do it it was called *Mr. Fox of Venice;* later, to my horror, it turned into *Anyone for Tennis;* and finally, for no reason that I could see, *The Honey Pot*. It was in fact an old play that Joe had found and optioned, based on Ben Jonson's *Volpone*. He had updated it to modern times, making Mr. Fox (*volpone* in Italian means "old fox") a modern man and using or reusing Ben Jonson's plot. If you think that last sentence is confusing, it has nothing on the confusion of the script. I left Joe to unravel himself and he said he would keep me informed of developments. It was then April and we did not actually start filming until early in the autumn of that year. To fill in time I did a couple of other things.

I went with *My Fair Lady* to Moscow for the film festival. There the film was shown in the Kremlin, where I made a speech from the stage, and the following day at a football stadium holding about fifty thousand people, who were for some reason immensely tickled by my description of my first day in Moscow. I said I had been to Lenin's tomb, and the shops. I never discovered what caused the howl of laughter. I was interviewed by the Soviet press about the Royal Court production of Chekhov's *Platonov,* which is seldom put on, and about which they seemed to know very little. I was struck by the difference of pace in Moscow. Perhaps because they are an eastern people, everything goes much slower. In restaurants one waited half an hour for service, when a bottle of vodka would be plonked on the table, and then a further half hour before the food turned up. And yet, at nine o'clock at night, women in their sixties were still working on the building sites, bricklaying.

That year too, while waiting for Joe, I was a judge at the Cannes Film Festival, which seemed to me very like representing one's country at the United Nations. The infighting between the Iron Curtain countries and the West was extensive. We found for example that during the secret ballots the Iron Curtain countries abstained from voting on films from the West, and would only vote in support of their own films. The chairman then insisted that every judge must give a verdict, every time—*oui* or *non*—and not abstain, whereupon the *nons* piled up against our films. The British went on all the same to win the top award, with that charming comedy *The Knack*.

The French were represented at the Festival by the writer Alain Robbe-Grillet, who plumped mischievously for a film

In Moscow for the film festival

with a very obvious story about two men going for a night out and picking up two tarts—Robbe-Grillet insisted that it had tremendous artistic merit, and lobbied everyone to vote for it. Also, to stress his point, he always went around accompanied by the two actresses who played the tarts. It was worth all the work entailed in watching thirty-six films in two weeks just to see M. Robbe-Grillet at work on the other judges with his tongue in both cheeks.

In August I was presented at Taormina in Sicily with the David di Donatello Award, Italy's Oscar, for both *My Fair Lady* and *The Yellow Rolls-Royce*. It was a fantastic ceremony which took place by moonlight in an old Greek amphitheater, now only a shell, on the heights above Taormina, overlooking Mount Etna. A long way from the stage of the Liverpool Playhouse.

Finally Joe was ready to start *The Honey Pot* with a cast of Maggie Smith, Susan Hayward, Capucine, and Cliff Robertson. A splendid lineup, but I am sure Joe would be the first to admit that it was not a happy experience. Once again I took a house on the Via Appia Antica, this one even more spooky than the one with the crypt, if such a thing was possible.

As I was making this film, another one was being prepared in Hollywood for me—another musical, based on Hugh Lofting's books for children, *Doctor Dolittle*.

CHAPTER TWELVE

Dolittle

EXCEPTING only that the hero did not fall in love with his leading lady, Chi-Chi the chimp, *Doctor Dolittle* had all the hallmarks of *Cleopatra*. It was rained out, it was moved from pillar to post, and poor Leslie Bricusse had far too much to do. He was responsible for dialogue and lyrics, as well as music. In one respect *Dolittle* outdid *Cleopatra:* it administered a near-fatal body blow to Twentieth Century–Fox's finances.

Hugh Lofting's Dr. Dolittle was a tiny round man with a very large W. C. Fields nose and bandy-legs—not quite the description I answer to—with the one great gift of being able to talk to animals literally in their own languages. Lofting started writing stories about him during the First World War, when he was in the trenches. He sent the first installments to his sons, his wife kept them, and after the war Lofting was persuaded to turn them into a book, which had a tremendous success and was followed by dozens of others. He could never have thought in his wildest dreams that his sweet gentle thoughts would one day cost Twentieth Century–Fox seventeen million dollars, which was never recouped.

We started shooting at Castle Combe in Wiltshire in August —which, as every Englishman knows, is the rainy season. Castle

Combe nestles in a valley which is one of the outstanding beauty spots of the west country, but they set about revamping it, at enormous expense, and much to the annoyance of the inhabitants. It was about a hundred miles from the sea, but Twentieth Century–Fox decided to turn it into a fishing village; they dug holes, and built dams, and imported water.

One gallant military gentleman was so incensed by this that he decided to wipe out Fox's plans, village and all. He acquired a quantity of dynamite and mined Castle Combe, setting detonators under several houses and under a garage. If it hadn't been for some careless talk in a pub in Bristol, which was overheard by a reporter, Castle Combe would have been rid of Fox, and of a score or so of its inhabitants.

We did Castle Combe one good turn, however. Since *Doctor Dolittle* was set at the turn of the century, we took down all the individual television aerials, replacing them with one communal aerial on the top of the hill. Reception was much improved, and in the evenings I think the village felt more kindly toward us. Nor was our name all mud with the keepers of shops and inns, who did a roaring trade of course. The people who were really out of countenance were the grander house owners, who weren't making any money out of us. The village boomed, and Fox took care when they left to remove all traces of their occupation.

It rained, though. It rained and rained, until the fields where the animals were kept turned into quagmires; and on the rare days of sunshine we began to learn, painfully, the problems of filming with animals.

One particularly beautiful morning, it was decided we would try shooting the squirrel sequence. Bricusse's script had the squirrel sitting on a bridge talking to Polynesia the parrot, with Dr. Dolittle listening to the conversation. A farmer had claimed to have a tame squirrel, and this was produced —in a cage, to our surprise. I didn't think it was tame, by any manner of means. It declined to sit on the bridge, and scratched at anyone who tried to hold it there, which was dangerous because squirrels can sometimes carry rabies. The handlers put on huge gloves and tried again, but the squirrel had no intention of keeping still, let alone sitting next to the parrot. The parrot was all right, he would just sit, and I, being a well-trained actor, did the same.

They tried next to wind little bits of wire around the squirrel's feet, and tether it to the bridge with small tacks, trusting to luck that the little creature would not injure itself. The sun was beating down, for the first time in days, and the squirrel grew more and more angry, but still they would not give up the shot. Lunch break came, and Richard Fleischer, the director, declared that he was going to see about sedating the squirrel. He called up the local vet, who said sedatives would kill the animal, and advised giving it a tot of gin.

So we invested in a bottle of gin and an old-fashioned fountain pen, and after lunch went back to the bridge. The squirrel was pinned down and given a fountain-penful of gin. This made it even madder, and it struggled so violently that it had to be put back in its cage. After a lot of head scratching they decided to try a further dose—maybe that would do the trick. And this time they did get a few seconds of film showing the squirrel on the bridge, nodding and swaying in a suspiciously drunken manner. They were so pleased with their success they thought they'd give it one more tot and get a picture of the squirrel with the parrot deep in conversation, just as the script ordered. The last shot did it: the squirrel crumpled and went to sleep, lying spread-eagled like a lizard. I hate to think what it felt like when it woke up. The next day it rained.

Eventually the powers that be conceded victory to the rain, and decided to leave dripping Wiltshire and rebuild the doctor's house, and part of the village, on Twentieth Century–Fox's ranch in California. Anything less like England would be hard to conceive of.

The studio set of Dr. Dolittle's study was not much larger than the living room in a nineteenth-century workman's cot-

"I spent over a year on *Doctor Dolittle* and my love for animals was at a remarkably low ebb." (20th Century–Fox)

tage, and unlike most sets the walls did not break away. I performed my first number, "The Vegetarian," in which I complained of my meatless diet and then realized I could not eat my friends, with some two hundred animals on the set with me, roaming around at will. The heat was intense, what with Todd-AO cameras, lights of all sorts and sizes, seventy crew members, and the animals aforementioned, not to speak of the pickup men rushing in with shovels and mops to clean up after the animals.

It was almost impossible to concentrate amid the confusion. At the end of the day, if anyone spoke to me suddenly, I would jump with fright, because I had been so long on the alert— not only for the small animals but for the large ones as well, who made no bones about walking on your feet or sitting on you. We had our casualties: one trainer was trampled by an elephant, another went down with a liver complaint caught from the chimps, a doe drank the contents of a painter's bucket and was laid up for a few days. I was insured by Fox for one million dollars, and wisely too, for I was bitten by a chimp, a Pomeranian puppy, a duck, and a parrot. Parrot bites can transmit a fatal disease, so I made haste to report to the nurse on set, who said cheerfully that there was nothing they could do for me, but would I please let them know if I did get a fever so that they could inform the authorities. I spent an uneasy week wondering if I might not turn into a parrot, and from then on kept the bird at arm's length.

Chi-Chi the chimp was a real joy when I first met her; she was sweet and affectionate, and never stopped kissing hands and cuddling me. But by the end of the year she had changed; so had I. Either she was as fed up with the film as I was, or perhaps she was entering into adolescence, when chimpanzees do become ugly. Her trainer had a theory that they suffer from permanent headache, because their skulls are too small for their brains! But then I sometimes worried about the trainers and wondered whether they had anything in their skulls at all. I was sitting on the set one day with Chi-Chi on my knee, get-

217

ting ready to do a number with the animals, and Chi-Chi was playing around with the papers on my desk, when her trainer, trying I suppose to be helpful, gave her a sudden wallop over the head. The little character turned on me, instead of on the trainer, and started to maul me, with teeth and claws and everything she had, out of sheer fright. I had a blazing row with that man and had him sent off the set—I could get along with Chi-Chi better without him.

The pace of work was inordinately slow. Each animal had its trainer, but before we started shooting a scene we had to clear the trainers off the set—whereupon the animals, naturally, wanted to find out where their trainers had got to and started wandering off in pursuit. We could not tether them, because they became restless and then angry. Matters were further complicated because we could never rehearse with the animals: we had to shoot each scene first time around. Once we had introduced a piece of action to the animal, it either liked it—and anticipated the camera, coming forward before we were ready for it—or it took against the idea and refused to come near us.

Rachel went to New York to make *Blithe Spirit* for television, and shortly after that the production of *Doctor Dolittle* adjourned to St. Lucia, one of the Windward Islands, in the Caribbean. By now it was November, and once again we found we had headed into the rainy season: not just English rain either, but five or six tropical storms a day, accompanied by thunder and lightning. Between storms the sun shone brilliantly and everything came out, including, alas, every fly and biting insect on the island.

I chartered a three-masted schooner, and we lived on board and on Sundays put the sails up and had some reasonable sailing: for a three-master you need a good wind. We took her around to the other side of the island and explored St. Lucia's walk-in volcano, climbing the shallow slopes until we reached the edge of a molten lake bubbling with sulfur geysers. Behind the volcano ran a clear and very tempting river, which harbored a tiny species of poisonous snail which was being investigated by an institute financed by an American foundation. The mouth of the river came out into the sea just where my scenes with the Giant Sea Snail were being filmed, and I picked my way about in the water rather gingerly, wondering which would get me first, the giant snail or the tiny poisonous one.

At that point I don't think I would have cared unduly if one of them had got me. The work with animals, the squabbling and backbiting behind scenes, and my own private troubles had among them already nearly finished me, and still I had the scenes to do with the seals. I had to feed these greedy and bone-stupid animals at sixty-second intervals from a bucket of fresh fish kept out of camera range, expecting at any moment to have one of them mistake my finger for a fish. All told I spent over a year on *Doctor Dolittle,* and my love for animals came to a remarkably low ebb.

Toward the end of this interminable epic we were working out at the Walt Disney ranch, finishing the number with the Pushmi-Pullyu, Lofting's invention—the double-headed llama. The weather again was not kind and I was sitting in my trailer under a large oak tree. On the oak was a plaque which read:

THE GOLDEN OAK
*Under this tree gold was first
discovered in California by
Don Francisco Lopez
9 March 1842*

It was a rugged valley in desert land now kept heavily watered by Disney so that the grass was green and peacocks walked on the lawns. But all around was the desert and one got an idea of what Don Francisco must have gone through a hundred and thirty-odd years ago to find gold in such a desolate spot. The legend goes that the man Lopez was sitting under this oak having some form of lunch. He pulled up a wild onion to eat and found gold particles in the soil. This event seemed

"They became restless and then angry." (20th Century–Fox)

to me as far removed from reality as the Pushmi-Pullyu double-headed llama and the dance I had to do with it. I suppose gold has always been a basic need. I couldn't think of any other reason why I was there.

I had to stay on many months after shooting had finished redoing my musical numbers for sound and a great deal of the dialogue. This was unusual but the locations had been so difficult that it had not been possible to record sound successfully.

While I was slaving away, I had contracted to do a film for Fox of Feydeau's *A Flea in Her Ear,* in Paris, and Doc Merman and Richard Zanuck, who were friends of mine and of Rachel's, offered her too a part in the film. This pleased her, the more so since another friend of hers, Rosemary Harris, was playing the leading lady.

"Would the Giant Sea Snail get me first?" (20th Century–Fox)

A Flea in Her Ear was written and first staged around the turn of the century, in the era known as La Belle Époque. The play had had a successful production at the National Theatre in London, and when Twentieth Century–Fox decided to make it into a movie, they sent me the script to read and I thought it was hilariously funny. But Gallic farce is a far call from English farce, and in retrospect I don't think Feydeau is workable on the screen. He designed his plays for the theatre, and in such a way that the eye must be able to rove around a whole stage, taking in first one outlandish situation and then another. That many of the effects did not work well in this film was not the fault of the playwright, nor of Jacques Charon, the marvelous French actor from the Comédie Française who directed us. Charon had not previously made films, but there are few directors who have had his ex-

221

perience, for he had spent years in the theatre and was accustomed to sketching out and giving his own interpretation of the performance he wanted from actors of sensibility. He was an expert in Feydeau farce, and I sometimes wished that he had been playing my part; he was so superb in demonstrating my role to me.

Rachel and I had hoped that working together on *Flea in Her Ear* would be a help to our marriage, but sadly it was not so. I think she had realized by then the extent of our mistake: she needed to be free, to lead her own life as an actress. The pattern of my life then was no help either, in fact it aggravated matters. We should have seen that our two life-styles would never fit, before we were married.

I suppose it is ridiculous to think that political attitudes don't affect behavior patterns. I have always tried to persuade myself that they shouldn't, but I have to concede by now that they do. I think of myself as a self-made man—I had no education to speak of, and inherited no money. My main incentive was to get out and get on, and not hang about like my father. I know from my two sons that Noel's incentive was to be as successful as I have been and Carey's incentive—although he admired my success—to be as different from me, in his own way, as he could. They both saw me, in their formative years, pushing and shoving my way through life, always with ups and downs, but with a degree of success, or at least of drive.

Rachel had no inherited incentives good or bad, but I think from her Welsh background inherited dislike and distrust of conventional mores. This surely has helped her to a unique accomplishment as a powerful actress, and I am terribly happy for her that she has now got many of the things she was working for and the success and reputation which she deserves.

As for me, after *A Flea in Her Ear* things seemed for a time to go from bad to worse. On the strength of the play of *Staircase* I had committed myself to make a film of it with Richard Burton, who had phoned me and said, "If you'll do it I'll do it," but when I got the film script I was totally sickened by what had been done with the story. The play, about two homosexuals, was acceptable and funny: the less said about the film script the better. The making of it was ghastly, the end result even more so.

It had been a long hard struggle since Kay died—a long haul of nine years in which it seemed to me that there had been more dark than light, at any rate in my private life. It was during rehearsals for a play called *The Lionel Touch* toward the end of 1969 that a new light began to shine for me in the person of Elizabeth, who is now my wife. The relationship took a long time in developing. For hours on end we used to sit and talk without any physical contact at all. I think we were both frightened of spoiling the joyous thing we had.

On the last night of the run of *The Lionel Touch* I had a private jet organized to take us to a "destination unknown." At Tangiers I had chartered a yacht to take us down the Atlantic coast of Morocco. It was the beginning of life with Elizabeth, and thank God there was once again a tomorrow to look forward to.

CHAPTER THIRTEEN

Now—and Elizabeth

ELIZABETH seems to encompass all the attractive qualities of all the women I have met. She is very beautiful, she enjoys life, she is not competitive. She is divinely feminine, very lazy, loathes exercise in God's fresh air. She is a strong person, mentally, and has strong convictions, which happily coincide with mine. She is, to me, the quintessence of Lady Mary in J. M. Barrie's *The Admirable Crichton,* only sexier.

It is only now that I have roots and a home with Elizabeth that I can understand the miseries and pains of my earlier, almost rootless existence. Actors lead terribly exposed lives. The effort of will that has to be exercised to get on the stage for a long performance is very great—or at least I find it so—and it is equally difficult to start a film part. It is a great support at these times to know at the back of your mind that you have a home, a background of permanence. I have only found this during the last years. I am obviously a very late developer.

After Elizabeth and I met and decided that we wanted to be together, there were a lot of hazards to be overcome. She was divorced from Richard Harris and had three sons, Damien, Jared, and Jamie, who would become my stepsons when we were married, but I had not yet obtained my divorce from Rachel.

Our first year together was spent entirely in each other's company. I did no work of any kind—a change for me, but I suppose I had taken such a beating professionally because of the bad choice of material since *My Fair Lady* that I wanted and needed to lie fallow. Anyway, my time was filled with Elizabeth, loving and living a new life.

We traveled a lot. I chartered the *Calisto,* the 300-footer that had taken us around the Moroccan coast, and we sailed around Italy, down the Yugoslavian coast, to Corfu and the Greek islands. From Dubrovnik on we had on board with us Helen and Trevor Howard. Trevor is an old and dear friend from our *French Without Tears* days.

Rhodes was the scene of a comedy that had all the elements of a classic silent-film farce. The harbor is quite well known as a difficult one to negotiate. One morning, after we had been there a day or two, we decided that we had had enough of the island and I asked the captain to get under way. It was about midday on a baking hot July day when we started to move.

We were all having a drink in the saloon when we looked out and saw to our amazement a restaurant called the Kontiki being towed out of the harbor with us. We had last seen it moored to the bank on the other side of the harbor. The people in the restaurant did not seem to notice and went on eating as though nothing was happening. Trevor went to the stern and tried to fend the restaurant off with his feet and I went up to the bridge and said, "Captain, you must have got our anchor crossed—we are taking a large restaurant out to sea with us." He hove to and came down to the stern deck. The Kon-tiki customers had begun to realize that something was wrong and were shouting and waving their arms, so all was bedlam. Our anchor chains were interlocked, and there we were, completely blocking the harbor mouth.

The rest of the afternoon was something that only Jacques

Tati could have visualized. No boats could go in or out of the harbor. Everybody was shouting. Finally, after about four hours, an enormous man appeared, by his chest measurement clearly a diver. Without any equipment, except that with which God had provided him, he dived and dived, coming up every few minutes with huge lengths of chain. By this time all the restaurant people were drunk, and we were very glad when we finally parted company. The captain was able at last to uncouple our boat, and we steamed off to derisive hoots from about ten other boats all waiting to get out of the harbor.

We ended the cruise at Athens having had a hilarious time all around the Greek islands—but nothing quite as spectacular as Rhodes.

I was barred by law from using my house in Portofino with Elizabeth and the boys until I had obtained my divorce, so we took a house in France belonging to Madame Auriol, the widow of the ex-President of France, at Cap Bênat in the South of France near Le Lavandou.

It was here I began to realize some of the complications of being a stepfather. It's a tough job. You have to find a level, you must not audition for the part—blood being thicker than water, you are very much at a disadvantage. I can only describe it as rather like being best man at a wedding: tactful affection is what is needed. Luckily the boys were quite young when I met Elizabeth—eight, ten, and twelve—so they began to take me vaguely for granted and even to enjoy my presence. Now that they are all four years older we have a special relationship—nothing to do with being stepfather and stepsons, but more like, to distort the meaning of a well-worn phrase, "just good friends."

A sense of timing is tremendously important in the theatre and I have always believed that it's the same in life. Elizabeth and I came together at exactly the right time. She had recently come through a very difficult few years, and I was in a very low state. There was an immediate bond between us, and although we talked (and still talk) endlessly I don't think

227

we have ever bored each other. It is strange now to think that in the past we quite often met casually at parties. But then she was married, and so was I. After her divorce she had a house in London that was full of fun and life. We started seeing each other and I used to go there often, and she always welcomed me with sweetness and warmth. It was then that I fell deeply in love with her and she literally restored me to life.

Elizabeth is very good with people and really enjoys entertaining. Whenever I've been away working it's wonderful coming back to find life going on with dogs and children and people all over the house. But we are equally and blissfully happy to be just on our own, and that's the supreme gift for any couple.

Recently we have bought a house in the South of France called Beauchamp, and Elizabeth and I love it very much. It is an old house, built over a hundred years ago, and has great beauty and tranquillity. Elizabeth has entirely redecorated it with a brilliant sense of color and style which is born in her. People sometimes wonder what style *is*. In a way it is like sex appeal—either you have it or you haven't. The most unlikely people have style, and it has nothing to do with class or upbringing, it is something God-given, a natural ease of mind and manner, a feeling for the past, relaxed and instinctive. Elizabeth has all of that.

I often wonder what would have happened to my life if I had not met Elizabeth when I did. Roads taken and not taken. How different it all would have been if in 1945 Hollywood had not called me, or I had refused the call; how different if I had accepted *The King and I* as a musical when it was offered to me and not done *My Fair Lady;* and the horrible thought of how different it would have been had Elizabeth not been there to bring me in from the rough waters where I was floundering to something infinitely better than I had ever known before.

During all this tricky time Elizabeth's mother and father

were most kind and understanding. Right from the start they were very warmhearted toward me and put no obstacles in our way. Elizabeth's father, David Rees-Williams, now Lord Ogmore, had had a brilliant legal and political career. We learned later on our trip around the world how much he had done and how much he was respected, especially by the people of Malaysia. Created a baron by Clement Attlee in the Labour Government of 1950, he later crossed the floor to become a Liberal, and had been President of the Liberal Party from 1963 to 1964.

I found that while I had been pulling my life together with Elizabeth a lot had been happening to the film industry. The "establishment," or the big studio setups, had collapsed with a dull and terrific thud. I had pretty well been in at the kill with *Cleopatra* at the cost of $35 million, *Doctor Dolittle* at the cost of $17 million, and two or three others amounting to at least $15 million between them.

There was now a new and interesting trend of independent productions, working with individual talent, for one picture at a time rather than half a dozen. This has in my opinion immeasurably improved the standard of the cinematic art. It is no longer an "industry" in quotes but artistic, industrious people's efforts to do what they want to do and say what they want to say. Gone are the pretty faces of the Fifties and Sixties. They have been replaced with anti-heroes and anti-heroines, and a reality that never existed before. Ugly they may be, but real they are, a great step forward toward naturalism, which has always been a great credo of mine. They look like people and not studio puppets from some dream world.

Because of this change I also felt an urge to get started on something new, but it seemed I was lumped in with the old brigade, a rather ironic turn of events as I had always been against them.

I turned my thoughts to television, actually a very unsatisfactory medium for actors. It is great for singers, stand-up comics, politicians, and chat shows in that order. All actors

of any size and dimension are brought down to the size of "The Box." However, I tried a couple of two-hour specials. One was the Chekhov play I had done at the Royal Court Theatre in 1960 called *Platonov,* which has not yet been shown in America, and the other was a part I had always wanted to play, *Don Quixote.*

More of this anon. . . . Although it was a big success both in England and America, I was personally disappointed to see how "The Box" diminishes all grandeur of scenery—the location in Spain on the plains of La Mancha was breathtaking. I always want to see around the corners of a television set, like a child in the theatre trying to see into the wings.

Between *Platonov* and *Don Quixote* my divorce came through and I was joyously free to marry Elizabeth. We were married on August 26, 1971, at Alan Lerner's house on Long Island. It was a very festive occasion with lots of friends and even more champagne. Elizabeth jokingly complains that up until a moment before the judge arrived to marry us I was on the phone giving last instructions for the cutting of *Platonov* for an American showing. But although my professional instincts certainly had revived, my mind was on other things. This time I had my fingers crossed.

After the wedding we returned to Portofino and had a very unconventional and happy honeymoon with the Ogmores, Elizabeth's three boys, and two of their cousins.

Summer holidays with Elizabeth are always rather like running a small hotel, so to give us some time to ourselves that autumn, I suggested that since I had to go to San Francisco for a film festival where they were doing a retrospective of all my films, we might keep going west and go around the world. This we decided was something we would both like to do.

On the whole, the week in San Francisco was fun. We were put up at the Mark Hopkins, in the presidential suite, and on October 2 I opened the film festival, introducing Princess

231

Wedding breakfast
(Steve Schapiro/Black Star)

Alexandra and her husband, the Hon. Angus Ogilvy, who were in San Francisco for British Fair Week.

The following day my retrospective began, with obsessively loyal fans sitting through extracts from or whole films of mine from nine in the morning until six o'clock. Then I appeared on the stage and answered questions from old and young—mostly polite, some interesting, like, Why had I always played kings and lords and on the whole upper-class characters? I was also asked by a young Siamese student whether I had meant to play "a silly king" in *Anna and the King of Siam*. I paused and said no, I had not meant to play a silly king; that I had thought him most serious, if slightly eccentric. But I felt obliged to remind the student that his present king had a daily radio show from the palace for an hour in the afternoon, when he played his saxophone to his subjects, and that I did not think that was silly either. Luckily I had been given this rather sweet piece of information sometime before.

In San Francisco I also opened the Highland Games with Elizabeth, as part of British Fair Week, and apparently took away with me by mistake, because I thought it had been handed to me, a statuettelike object which was supposed to be one of the prizes for the large Scottish athletes who toss the caber, fling the hammer, and other such things. The next day after the Games were over I met Angus Ogilvy, who told me of my error. When the Princess came to give out the honors there was one short—he said it had made his entire stay.

On October 4 we had our second typhoid and cholera and other shots and took a plane for Honolulu. On our second day Elizabeth and I were asked to lunch with Clare Boothe Luce, an interesting example of the American career woman whom I had not encountered before. A very clever and entertaining woman, she seemed a piquant combination of masculine forcefulness and feminine guile. She totally ignored Elizabeth, who was, I must say, looking extremely young and beautiful, but who also has an enormously agile mind. Mrs. Luce concentrated solely on the male members of the luncheon party.

We left Honolulu for Hong Kong via Tokyo on October 13, and had not been airborne for more than half an hour when Elizabeth showed me a small item in the Honolulu paper. There was a typhoon over Luzon, moving north, and another in the Hong Kong area, also moving north over the China Sea. I sent a nervous message up to the captain asking about Hong Kong, and got a reply saying Hong Kong was all right; it was Tokyo—our next stop!—that was the worry.

We slept fitfully, drank, and ate. Then we crossed the International Date Line. I felt nothing, but discussed whether the fact that it was now Thursday, instead of Wednesday, might not affect the typhoons. One would think that a typhoon would realize it was late in some way in reaching its destination and be so damned ashamed it would die down, or go faster hoping to catch up. Elizabeth gave me a long look. Half an hour out of Tokyo, at 40,000 feet, we hit the typhoon. Our descent through swirling black cloud was memorable, and when we landed—safely, thank God—at three o'clock in the afternoon it was pitch dark. We then had to take off again, in another plane with a special pilot for the job of landing at Hong Kong's particularly difficult airport, climb up again through the edge of the typhoon, and fly on to our destination.

Hong Kong, where we stayed five days, is of course a complete anachronism. But as one says about other places in the Far East, "You can see what it must have been like." One cannot fail to be struck by the visible contrast between the very rich and the very poor.

Probably the most interesting and energetic of the rich Chinese who benefit from the general absence of unions in Hong Kong is Run Run Shaw, which I think is a graphic endearment for his real name, Rein Shaw. He very kindly asked Elizabeth and me to visit his film studios, where he makes forty full-length feature films a year for the Oriental market. He has an empire, with cinemas all over the world, not just in the East but in every western city that has an Oriental quarter. There is no limit on working hours for the actors, technicians, writers, producers, and others at his studios. He has built large, modern flatlets for his employees to live in so that they will not be late on the set. If one of them is lucky enough to be married with a family, he gets larger accommodations.

Run Run Shaw is proud of his achievement. He said to me, "Of course I could never do this if there were unions," and smiled. He has a thin, clever, clear face and I must say I liked him. On the other hand I might not like him so much if I were an Oriental actor, technician, or director.

For the rest our stay in Hong Kong was not very eventful. We were advised by our rich Chinese acquaintances to go to what they called the "pigeon restaurant." It sounded divine, so off we went. It was very large, very dirty, reached through a disgusting garden full of cages and feathers, with an overpowering smell of burning flesh. The pigeons produced for us to eat were defeathered, admittedly, but had obviously been burnt alive because they came in with necks, heads, and beaks erect. When we asked the waiter if he could take the heads away he looked at us first with incredulity and next with glee, because that is what the Chinese consider the best bit—beak, eyes, the lot, of the baby pigeon.

Was Hong Kong really the place of which everybody had said to me, "You must go, you must see it"? See what? The *Queen Elizabeth* lying a total derelict, hoping to become a university? Millions of Chinese rushing like nobody ever rushes in Times Square? Poverty, filthy food, sleazy joints only for sailors? Old men in the ladder streets hammering at long-broken transistor sets that would never work again, even at little bits of tin—anything, it seems, to keep their arms moving senselessly? Little boys and mangy dogs? It seemed to me there were more dogs than usual in such places. Could this be a hangover from the English?

234

Every schoolboy has a romantic image of the Orient. I had it. I dreamed of the South Seas, of coral islands and clear water and colored fish and jungles. Perhaps if I had gone there when I was a boy, my dreams would have come true; but not now—except at our next stop, Kuala Lumpur and the Malay Peninsula: there it still exists.

Flying down the Malay Peninsula you pass over miles and miles of impenetrable jungle, and one imagines the wild animal life, the tigers, herds of elephants, still to be found there. Finally you come in over the Cameron Highlands and down over total jungle to the runway at Kuala Lumpur.

Our welcome at Kuala Lumpur was extremely warm and we were wined and dined most cordially. Elizabeth was the toast of the town. David Ogmore had got to know the Malaysians when as a young man he had gone out to practice law in Penang. The interesting structure of the Malaysian constitution is largely his work. When it was being drawn up there was a lot of argument about which of all the rulers of the separate states was to be monarch of the new state. The problem was solved quite brilliantly by my father-in-law by dividing the responsibilities of the monarchy among the individual rulers, each of whom was to serve a term of five years as monarch. Under that monarch, who has to be as nonpartisan as our own royal family, the country is run by a prime minister —Tun Abdul Razak, whom we met. Elizabeth had known him since she was a young girl and met him at her father's house in London when he was in England studying for the Bar, and it was a very happy and festive reunion.

Kuala Lumpur has an old town, mostly Chinese. The British section was built in Victorian times, the railway station being the grandest piece of architecture by far, as was usual in those days. The Malaysian Parliament buildings are modern but very well planned, in a pleasant park. We saw the batik factory, where they make beautiful and unusual prints with hot wax and various combinations of dyes. By contrast we visited a hospital compound to which sick tribesmen from the jungle are flown by helicopter for treatment. The sick man arrives not alone but with his entire family, who will not be parted from him, and when he is better insists on being flown back at once to the jungle: the tribesmen hate our way of life and it occurred to me that their primitive jungle is no more terrifying than the jungle which we are pleased to call "civilization."

Our last stop in the Far East was at Bangkok, now a vast, straggling, American-type town where skyscrapers mingle with small hovels and the general air is one of dejection. The famous Oriental Hotel is still there, entirely modernized of course, but still boasting a Somerset Maugham suite and a Noël Coward suite. And there is a little of the old Bangkok left by the river. The palaces and the temples are very beautiful, and it was strange to recognize it all, even to the ornamental trees cut in strange shapes, from the very accurate sets built by Twentieth Century–Fox for *Anna and the King of Siam* in 1945.

Having myself played King Mongkut in that film, I was amused to find when we arrived in Bangkok that it was the anniversary of Mongkut's son, Chulalongkorn, who had been called The Great. The next day we drove off early to see his statue which had been very highly decorated. The Temple of the Green Buddha was open, as it rarely is, so we went in. Elizabeth had to take her shoes off and as she was wearing no stockings, I was worried about all those diseases you can catch through the soles of your feet. I had socks on! However, all was well—unless of course the incubation period is the longest ever.

The following day, rather thankfully, we boarded a flight for London. We were to make only one stop, at Teheran. We landed there perfectly, went into the lounge, came out, sat down in the aircraft—and nothing happened. They had got the flaps down, but could not get them up again. After many consultations we were finally put on another flight—a smallish aircraft, packed, stopping at Athens, Vienna, Brussels . . .

The heat, three broken ribs and Spanish horseflies made the shooting of *Don Quixote* a nightmare
(Gordon Moore/Scope Features)

We arrived back in London stretcher cases, but we had actually been around the world, and we felt quite proud of ourselves, and very much in love.

Early in 1972 I started preparing the script for *Don Quixote* with the director, Alvin Rakoff. It took a long time to devise a coherent story line out of the two vast volumes, and at one time the BBC felt they had bitten off more than they could chew. However, we made some cuts in the expenses and were finally to start shooting the film that summer in Spain.

Before I left a nasty thing happened. Elizabeth and I went to Portofino to inspect some land I had bought to enlarge the property. In my excitement I slipped on one of the terraces, hurtled down about six more, and landed hard on my right side. For a while I thought I was just bruised, but the next morning found no way of getting out of bed except by rolling carefully onto the floor. I had broken three ribs. There was no way of postponing the shooting of the film—everything was ready to go on the plains of La Mancha. So I got myself strapped up and proceeded with Elizabeth to Madrid.

It was not funny, in fact it was hell. I still don't know how I got through it. Elizabeth was with me, thank goodness, but it wasn't much fun for her. The accommodations were very primitive; the horseflies looked to me the size of small birds— one was found in my beard just before a scene. The roads were appalling on my ribs, let alone my horse Rosinante, who by the end of the day was covered in blood from horsefly bites. To mount him I had to climb up a ladder and then be lowered gently into the saddle. The armor I had to wear did not help my condition either. It was rather like having violent tooth-ache in your side for about three months.

At last, in spite of the rough treatment, my ribs healed —just as I finished the film. With the heat, the ribs, and the horseflies, tempers got very frayed, but Alvin Rakoff was extremely patient with me and we ended up the best of friends in spite of everything. I shall never forget the beauty of the

Don Quixote and Elizabeth

landscape and the whole experience of playing a part I had always wanted to play.

By now I was back in my stride and going full tilt, thanks to Elizabeth. I was anxious to return to the theatre as soon as possible, if only to prove to myself that I wasn't as bad as *The Lionel Touch* had made me feel. I obtained from the estate of the Italian author Luigi Pirandello the rights to his play *Henry IV,* a play about madness. Although acclaimed as a twentieth-century masterpiece, it has rarely been performed in English. Its enormous central role is that of a modern man who believes he is an eleventh-century emperor. It had not been seen on the London stage since 1927.

In December of 1972 I left for New York to present *The Emperor Henry IV* (as it was called in America) under the banner of Sol Hurok. Clifford Williams was directing the play. I was to do a sixteen-week tour of North America, playing Toronto, Los Angeles, Boston, Washington, and a six-week season in New York. Elizabeth again heroically came with me.

The play went very well and the American audiences loved it. It was an exhilarating tour, although hard work. The worst hop was closing in Los Angeles on Saturday and opening three thousand miles away in Boston on Monday.

I have a great affection for Boston, because in November, 1973, I returned there to be presented with the honorary degree of Doctor of Humane Letters at Boston University. It was a very impressive ceremony and a great honor for an actor to receive an honorary doctorate. I was extremely delighted that America should reward me in this way for all the work I had done both in films and in the theatre in their country. I had to make a speech and was quite petrified under these solemn circumstances. Being at the podium on a platform surrounded by begowned professors seemed a long way away from *Charley's Aunt.* I had written a speech with great care and just managed to stutter my way through it. I pinched quite a lot from a speech I had found that Sir Henry Irving had made on receiving an honorary degree at Edinburgh

In Pirandello's *Henry IV* (Martha Swope)

Dr. Harrison with President Silber at Boston University
(Boston University Photo Service)

University. It was great stuff, but I told everybody it wasn't mine because it sounded vaguely out of date.

The tour had continued successfully, finishing at the Ethel Barrymore Theatre in New York, where years before I had played in *Bell, Book and Candle*. I returned to London at the end of April, 1973, Elizabeth having gone on ahead of me. I then began in earnest to write this autobiography. I had done a lot of preliminary work before the tour, but now I retired to Portofino and got down to the strange job of trying to recall my life.

Early the following year my labors were interrupted to begin rehearsals in London for the Pirandello play. The Bernard Delfont Organization were putting it on for me at Her Majesty's Theatre in the Haymarket.

It was, I suppose, one of the worst times in recorded history to start doing anything in London because we had strikes, a three-day working week, hardly any light or heat, and a general election looming to compete with the opening night. However, to my great joy we began (in semidarkness) to perhaps the best set of notices I had ever received from the London critics. The production had a new cast and a new set. Also, Clifford Williams and I had reinserted certain parts of the play that had not been performed in America, which made the redoing of it even more of a challenge.

I must say the success of this obscure and brilliant play has given me a great sense of fulfillment. I felt it was one of the few untouched near-masterpieces of the twentieth century. That is why I personally optioned it and I am delighted that so many people have had the opportunity to see it.

There is, of course, no retiring age in our profession, and although I have just completed fifty years in the theatre I am as full of plans for ventures on the stage and for films and television as I have ever been. By the time this book is published no doubt some will have taken shape and some will have bitten the dust. Fifty years' experience is no guarantee against abject failure—or against sudden success.

My eldest granddaughter, Katharine, gave her first interview to the press at the age of eleven. She was reported as saying, "The difference between Grandfather and myself is that I'm going to be a serious actress." Well, I know what she meant and I took and take it as a compliment, however left-handed. Styles change but truth in acting doesn't. I've always tried to be the sort of actor who works from the inside out to develop a character. It takes time and concentration, but the aim is to make the performance *look* easy so that the audience may even think, I could do that. It is possible by concentrating on the outside of a character—the walk, the voice, the accent, the makeup, the wardrobe—to give a dazzling performance, but it will rarely move an audience unless the inward portrayal is true. I'm very serious in this respect; and whatever the final verdict on me as an actor may be, I'm hopeful that the seriousness of my intention will be accepted.

Family party: (left to right) Simon Harrison, Jared Harris, Jamie
Harris, Elizabeth, Harriette Harrison, R.H., Damien Harris

How does an actor know when he is good? He himself is often the worst judge, and few critics have a clear idea, any more than the public has. What criteria can you apply? Public esteem? Riches and fame? Not likely. But poverty and obscurity are no yardsticks either. Success? Ah yes, but how successful? Has he made it internationally? Has he made it artistically? And so it goes on, in the minds of all actors, struggling and successful. Nobody can tell them when they have truly made it. An achievement written down, or painted on canvas, a decision that makes history, a scientific discovery, a journey to the moon—these can be pinpointed and appraised. The actor, who is on earth to entertain all those people who do things great and small, cannot measure himself until he realizes that that is the full aim of his job: not to dictate or to preach, not to be too damn clever for his own ends, or think he has anything more important to do than, simply, to entertain.

I hoped when I started this book that I might find out something about myself in the process of writing it. I'm not altogether flattered by the results of my research, but when sometimes I am asked whether I would change my life if I were able to live it over again, I have to answer no. I'd almost certainly make a worse hash of it the second time around. There have been some black times, but I've got through them as best I can and it's true that those who experience great unhappiness have an added capacity for enjoying and being grateful for happiness when it comes.

I do regret one major misconception. I had always believed that actors should be married to actresses. Absolute rubbish—actors should be married to wives. Of course I am lucky that Elizabeth has always been mixed up in the theatre and studied at the Royal Academy of Dramatic Art for some time. She has quite definite ideas about what she likes and dislikes in the theatre and those feelings happily coincide nearly always with my own. But I am happier still that she decided early on to give it up and is not ashamed to have "Housewife" written in her passport. She is a mother as well as a wife and I love that side of her too. She adores her sons and I enjoy watching her adore them.

I now find myself with more time to take up old friendships, to make new ones, and to develop new interests in the outside world. I look with love and admiration at my younger son, Carey, who runs three careers simultaneously—he's a playwright of great skill, a lecturer at Essex University, and a registered goat-breeder. I'm as proud of that as indeed I am of Noel's great success in the entertainment world both in Britain and America.

In the last analysis, it is Elizabeth who has given my life dimension and meaning. Elizabeth and I share hopes and anxieties, pleasures and alarms, fair weather and squalls. I am thankful that there are no dull moments for us, and Elizabeth is the major factor in the unending variety that characterizes our life together.

Each day for us is different, every moment of the day an event, frequently unexpected, often disconcerting, always intriguing.

Unlike Henry Higgins, I didn't "just let a woman in my life"—I asked Elizabeth to share it, and she was brave enough to say yes.

Rex Harrison—
Plays and Films 1924-74

Film titles are given in lightface italics.

1924–7 Liverpool Repertory, in **Thirty Minutes in a Street, Old English Links, Doctor Knock, Gold, A Kiss for Cinderella, Milestones, Abraham Lincoln**

1927–34 Toured in **Charley's Aunt, Cup of Kindness, Potiphar's Wife, Alibi, Richard III, The Chinese Bungalow, After All, Other Men's Wives, For the Love of Mike, Mother of Pearl, The Great Game, The Road House, The School for Scandal, The Wicked Flee**

1930   **Getting George Married,** Everyman, London

1931   **The Ninth Man,** Prince of Wales, London

1933   **Another Language,** Lyric, London

1934   **No Way Back,** Whitehall, London
        Our Mutual Father, Piccadilly, London
        Anthony and Anna, Fulham, London
        Get Your Man

1935   **Man of Yesterday,** St. Martin's, London
        Short Story, Queen's, London
        Leave It to Blanche
        All at Sea

1936   **Charity Begins—,** Aldwych, London
        Sweet Aloes, Booth Theatre, New York
        Heroes Don't Care, St. Martin's, London
        Storm in a Teacup

1936-7 **French Without Tears,** Criterion, London
1937 *Men Are Not Gods*
St. Martin's Lane (Sidewalks of London in USA)
1938 *School for Husbands*
Over the Moon
1939 **Design for Living,** Haymarket, London
The Citadel
The Silent Battle
Ten Days in Paris
Night Train to Munich (Night Train in USA)
1940 *Major Barbara*
1941-2 **No Time for Comedy,** Haymarket, London
1944 *Journey Together* (RAF film)
1945 *I Live in Grosvenor Square*
Blithe Spirit
The Rake's Progress (Notorious Gentleman in USA)
1946 *Anna and the King of Siam*
1947 *The Ghost and Mrs. Muir*
The Foxes of Harrow
1948 *Unfaithfully Yours*
Escape
1948-9 **Anne of the Thousand Days,** Shubert, New York
1950 **The Cocktail Party,** New Theatre, London
1950-1 **Bell, Book and Candle,** Ethel Barrymore, New York
1951 *The Long Dark Hall*
1952 **Venus Observed,** New Century, New York
The Fourposter
1953 **The Love of Four Colonels,** Shubert, New York
Main Street to Broadway
1954 *King Richard and the Crusaders*
1954-5 **Bell, Book and Candle,** Phoenix, London
1955 **Nina** (directed), Haymarket, London
The Constant Husband
1956-8 **My Fair Lady,** Mark Hellinger, New York; Drury Lane,
London
1958 **The Bright One** (directed), Winter Garden, London
The Reluctant Debutante
1959 **The Fighting Cock,** ANTA, New York

1960 **Platonov,** Royal Court, London
      Midnight Lace
1961 **August for the People,** Edinburgh Festival and Royal
      Court, London
1962 *The Happy Thieves*
1963 *Cleopatra*
1964 *My Fair Lady*
1965 *The Yellow Rolls-Royce*
      The Agony and the Ecstasy
1967 *The Honey Pot*
      Doctor Dolittle
1968 *A Flea in Her Ear*
1969 **The Lionel Touch,** Lyric, London
      Staircase
1971 *Platonov* (television film)
1972 *Don Quixote* (television film)
1973–4 **The Emperor Henry IV,** Ethel Barrymore, New York
1974 **Henry IV,** Her Majesty's, London

Index

251

INDEX

INDEX

INDEX